# Research Through, With and As Storying

*Research Through, With and As Storying* explores how Indigenous and non-Indigenous scholars can engage with storying as a tool that disassembles conventions of research. The authors explore the concept of storying across different cultures, times and places, and discuss principles of storying and storying research, considering Indigenous, feminist and critical theory standpoints. Through the book, Phillips and Bunda provide an invitation to locate storying as a valuable ontological, epistemological and methodological contribution to the academy across disciplines, arguing that storying research gives voice to the marginalised in the academy.

Providing rich and interesting coverage of the approaches to the field of storying research from Aboriginal and white Australian perspectives, this text seeks to enable a profound understanding of the significance of stories and storying. This book will prove valuable for scholars, students and practitioners who seek to develop alternate and creative contributions to the production of knowledge.

**Louise Gwenneth Phillips** is an academic in the School of Education at the University of Queensland, Brisbane, Australia.

**Tracey Bunda** is Professor and Head of the College for Indigenous Studies, Education and Research at the University of Southern Queensland, Toowoomba, Australia.

# Research Through, With and As Storying

**Louise Gwenneth Phillips
and Tracey Bunda**

Routledge
Taylor & Francis Group
LONDON AND NEW YORK

First published 2018 by Routledge

2 Park Square, Milton Park, Abingdon, Oxfordshire OX14 4RN
52 Vanderbilt Avenue, New York, NY 10017

*Routledge is an imprint of the Taylor & Francis Group, an informa business*

First issued in paperback 2020

*British Library Cataloguing-in-Publication Data*
A catalogue record for this book is available from the British Library

*Library of Congress Cataloging-in-Publication Data*
A catalog record for this book has been requested

ISBN: 978-1-138-08949-5 (hbk)
ISBN: 978-0-367-60723-4 (pbk)

DOI: 10.4324/9781315109190

We dedicate this book to our ancestors who gave us the gift of stories – the gift to story. And to those who have storied before us, to those who inspire us and nurture us, we hold deep thanks and gratitude. We remain as one with you and with stories.

# Contents

# Foreword

## Through storying, may we never be still

From our earliest memories, elders family members and friends tell stories that nurture us, challenge us and inform us of beautiful realities of the stars in the sky that guide us in spiritual and earth-bound journeys. Stories also warn us about harsh pain brought on by racism, assault and war. Louise Phillips and Tracy Bunda come "together" in order "two-gather" shared meanings. They remind us that when all voices are being heard through storying, regardless of positionality, we can have hope and create "guide ropes" to nurture relationships, form authentic collaborations and energise actions to support humanness in all our encounters. The language and metaphors are vivid throughout this book, and the authors evoke a range of dynamic and passionate emotions.

This work with storying, courageously led by Phillips and Bunda, addresses the human meaning making involved in the passion to tell stories and the thirst to receive the stories. The webs of connection among academic research, pedagogy and influence open the possibility for new methodologies, new positionality and new theorising that are inclusive rather than exclusive. Of course, stories do take many shapes as the authors here acknowledge and honour. And the intended sharing of meaning of stories is always contingent upon the context in which the stories are shared, the relationships among the storying-givers and the storying-receivers and, of course, the language used to share the stories. Translation of stories is not always perfect, to be sure, and this is more dire and consequential within contexts of exploitation, colonialism, war and oppression.

Stories support our changing norms of knowledge delivery and exchange and mantles of expert roles among all participants. Stories are often transgenerational. Educators are beginning to acknowledge the importance of multigenerational learning through stories. Thankfully, Indigenous peoples all over the world have rich traditions that have supported perseverance with storying, and many in academia are just beginning to be tutored in the knowledge and humanness passed down through the storying practices and are just beginning to learn of the power.

For years I've learned from participants in storying research whose wisdom and experience puts my own knowledge in the shadows. Often muses – knowledgeable and informative – come to us in the personas of learners from all ages and all backgrounds. Expertise is seen in the eyes and gestures of a 3-year-old, the cryptic words of a 90-year-old elder from the Anishinabe people in Northern Minnesota, a Nigerian woman who escaped from gaol in Libya, and an unaccompanied minor seeking asylum in the United Kingdom.

As the authors say, "humanness is inextricably tied to the larger projects of justice and love." And speaking of our projects with storying that spread wings and webs across many types of activities, theorising and analysis of research, we do see contention and dismay. And we are charged with the task of being courageous in the new frontiers of knowledge production. And what in many white, positivist cultures seems to be an oxymoron, research must begin with what the community being researched wants. Many of us believe research should always be a collaboration that certainly includes insiders as guides. It cannot be a space that only advances the careers of white academics. It must be a space that value adds to Aboriginal communities, communities of migration, communities of poverty, communities who don't use dominant languages and communities whose people hold unique values and life choices.

Phillips and Bunda acknowledge that the technologies and apparatuses that operate in the academy that focus on scientific and empirical imperatives are limiting and not inclusive. And the brave authors don't stop there. This limiting focus in the academy, they propose, could be the "binds that tie us" to the academy but often prohibit study of "values – within a set of guide ropes – that remind us of our humanness."

The authors show us multiple ways that storying is transformative whilst also highlighting the joyfulness of the work in its making. And as with most transformations, there is a complicated mix of struggle, even trauma, and uncertainty along with the joy.

We, at the end of 2017, are reeling from terrible political stories of war, displacement, trauma, migration, stories of decades of sexual assault and abuse, and even in Southern California a story from a 4-year-old girl saying to her preschool teacher, "La migra [immigration agency in the US] took my dad. I'm leaving soon to be with my dad. Mom said." Yet, the authors take the position that "stories are alive and in constant fluidity as we story with them. In research, we see storying as sitting and making emergent meaning with data slowly over time through stories." This gives us hope for our human condition; stories do support our humanness.

This work resonates for me because stories have supported much research that problematises the neocolonial roots of our conceptions of children and families in my own country and around the world. Stories highlight institutional systems, the pedagogies, the assessments and daily life realities affecting learners who have been colonised, who are immigrants and who are currently migrating through uncertain global landscapes. Many of our participants, both children and adults, are living and studying in California and they bring with them generations of family stories, knowledge, linguistic perspectives and lived experiences from Indigenous communities from the Oaxaca region of Mexico and from Central America. Their specific family experiences in multilingual contexts, with multigenerational knowledges, critical conceptualizations of place and matters of concern (Latour, 2004), were born, in part, from their experiences in their homelands. We see evolving theoretical stances to early childhood work with children and families based upon a third space that combines aspects of the homeland and the communities where they now live.

We do learn from each other's experiences. We learn from children. We learn from colleagues we have yet to meet. Wisdom from artists, political activists and folk tales helps frame the complex nature of our work. Ortiz (2001) explains that his people have been living a history of questions for 500 years. He documents that folk tales and art are the ways Indigenous people speak truth to power. In "The Story of Questions" the conversation between Subcomandante Marcos and the elder Antonio is about Zapata, a leader of the Mexican Revolution who was of Indigenous ancestry and spoke Nahuatl. He says, "But it is also not about Zapata. It is about what shall happen. It is about what shall be done" (Ortiz, 2001, p. 51). The folk tale ends with the following:

> This is how the true men and woman learned that questions are for walking, not for just standing around and doing nothing. And since then, when true men and women want to walk, they ask questions. When they want to arrive, they take leave. And when they want to leave, they say hello. They are never still.

May we never be still, with stories supporting us.

Elizabeth P. Quintero
California State University, Channel Islands

## References

Latour, B. (2004). Why has critique run out of steam? From matters of fact to matters of concern. *Critical Inquiry*, *30*(Winter), 225–248. Chicago, IL: The University of Chicago.

Ortiz, S. (2001). Essays. In *Subcomandante Marcos, folktales of the Zapatista revolution*. El Paso, TX: Cinco Puntos Press.

# Preface

This book has arisen from our working relationship and deep desire to share our work and interest in storying. We hope it encourages transformation, whilst also giving high value to the joyfulness of storying. First though, we must locate ourselves, and then have a discussion of how we came together. So that you may know who is who, Louise is speaking in *italics*, whilst Tracey is not.

In Aboriginal communities, naming oneself through defining, in Aboriginal vernacular, who is your mob and where does that mob come from, what country, is protocol. To this extent then, I name myself as Ngugi/Wakka Wakka and respectfully follow both matrilineal and patrilineal lines of descent. My professional identity is very much tied to my work in Aboriginal and Torres Strait Islander higher education which I have undertaken for last three decades.

*I am a white fifth-generation Australian who has worked with Aboriginal early childhood communities since the late 1980s, with the Kameygal peoples of Eora nation, with the Dunghutti peoples, and more recently with Aboriginal peoples of the 35 nations who were relocated to Wakka Wakka country. For the last 15 years (and the first 16 years of my life), I respectfully walk, work and live on the country of Jagera, Yuggera and Turrbal peoples and have recently nestled a home in Tar'au-nga (Taringa; place of stones).*

*In August 2014, when I was the cochair of the Postgraduate Research Conference Committee at my institution, we invited Tracey to give the keynote address to foreground Aboriginal Australian ontologies, epistemologies and methodologies. I was relatively fresh from the completion of my own PhD and was honoured by this invitation. In not knowing the audience, I was hoping that the appeal of stories was universal. With this presumption tucked under my arm, off I went and delivered an address that fundamentally argued that the PhD is a story – albeit a large storytelling of people, events, histories, lived lives, juxtapositions, contradictions, contentions and compulsions.*

*Tracey intimately shared her parents' lived stories of enforced mission incarceration – of separation from family from a young age and ongoing daily lived encounters of racism illustrated with family photos and pertinent intersections with critical race theory.* I urged that the doctoral study is a story that connects back to the student as storyteller, as the conduit for other stories, stories that are theoretically bound because you make it so or because the story theoretically does so for itself. In the address, I told stories of my family but I also told why I tell stories of my family.

*I was emceeing the event and recall a profound silence when Tracey's address ended, as we sat holding the pain in her stories. Through Tracey's poetic storytelling of her family's lived experiences, we came to know, more intimately, the legacies of colonisation.* Stories of my family were an honouring of those who had passed.

*A few months later we were both at an Australian Association of Research in Education meeting. I was representing a Narrative Inquiry research group and I spoke of a desire to use the more inclusive term* story. *Tracey gave a very affirming "I'm with you" response, which I treasured.* Not long after, Louise then asked me to join a research application that she facilitated (human rights education and children's citizenship) and though our application was not successful we had the opportunity to work together again. *The following year, I invited Tracey to present a paper in a symposium titled Storying and Self in Narrative Research at the Australian Association of Research in Education conference.* These connections also allowed us to strengthen our relationship. *In the writing of my paper and the presentation of our papers for that symposium I began to think, "There is a book here."* And by the time she asked to share in the writing of this book, I did not have any hesitation. *And so began months and months of talking and writing about, through and with stories . . .* Stories are and stories we be.

*I want to make clear that my invitation to Tracey to coauthor a book on storying was motivated by her connection and affirmation of story and storying, not to tokenistically tick a box of including Aboriginal knowledges on storying.* This is true. Contributing to this book allows me to balance out all the separate roles I occupy within the university – manager, administrator, advocate, mentor, academic, researcher and scholar. And if I am strategic, storying connects back into each. It's head down, *boonthi* up, write the book, because you want to and because you can.

*Every day I am grateful for this opportunity for us to cowrite on what is dear to us both. I am acutely aware and sensitive to the racialised tensions in Australia, and for Tracey to collaborate with a white person is a confronting step of trust when it is known, and deeply embodily known, that whitefullas "fuck you over" through theft of children, land and knowledges and ongoing subjugated positioning. I never want to add to this ongoing intergenerational pain, though I am aware that simply my white presence can stir the pain and ill thought, through expressions that may be heard and received as harmful. Knowing this, I tread carefully, consultatively, transparently and kindly. Tracey and I meet, talk, share stories, share gifts and share homes. And I ask questions and permissions of Tracey about my expression and direction frequently.* Again, this is true. For sure, there are said-out-loud agreements in forming a collaboration . . . with some silent/unspoken bits. The presence of racialised spaces – including our own writing space – does not mean that as an Aboriginal person, I do not have agency. There are no troublings that we cannot talk through. Having said that, I also acknowledge your respect of me and Aboriginal matters and hopefully you can see that this is reciprocated.

*We have written this book on Google Docs (no product endorsement intended) so that our writing is visible to each other throughout the process. I am aware that I have no control over how readers receive this work, but I hope that you understand my position, as one of deeply supportive, empathetic and respectful of Indigenous peoples, and that I have worked closely and kindly with Aboriginal Australian people for many years. I am also aware that many readers will look to this book to hear Tracey's stories and Aboriginal knowings, because Aboriginal Australians are a minority voice rarely heard. I humbly accept a side position: a small gesture of unconditional surrender that broadly white Australia has lacked courage to enact, yet is required for Indigenous sovereignty (Nicolacopoulos & Vassilacopoulos, 2014).* How many fora have we now entered where our shared voice on storying has been underheard by those within the audience who want to fetishize and hold a fascination to only the Indigenous within our work? Blah! Some days you have to take the objectifying gaze of individual whiteness and twist its neck so it will look hard at itself. You are correct; there are no guarantees for the ways in which we want to be seen and heard. Our methodology for working together is careful and considered, courageous and a work in progress that is not taken for granted. Hopefully readers will want to surrender to our words and thoughts in this book on research through, with and as storying, and be encouraged to add, develop and create their own storied research work.

In being true to the relationality of story and storying, we introduce authors that we refer to by their full names, then subsequently refer to them by first or full names. We see such as a more respectful way to refer to others.

## Reference

Nicolacopoulos, T., & Vassilacopoulos, G. (2014). *Indigenous sovereignty and the being of the occupier: Manifesto for a white Australian philosophy of origins.* Melbourne: Re.Press.

# Acknowledgements

We, foremost, acknowledge Aboriginal Australians for sustaining the longest living culture through story, storytelling and storying. We are honoured to create this work emplaced on the country of such extraordinary legacy.

We would like to acknowledge the insightful review of this book by Kathryn Gilbey and Jenny Ritchie, and the generosity of Elizabeth Quintero in writing the foreword and for the so amenable, behind-the-scenes assistance provided by Catherine Delzoppo.

# 1 Beginning stories and storying

## Together/two-gather through storying

We have a deep desire for our research through, with and as storying to be transformative whilst also giving high value to the joyfulness of the work in its making. Our work, as academics, is situated in the field of education: for Tracey, in Aboriginal and Torres Strait Islander education, and for Louise, in early childhood and arts education. Our (and the *our* here stands with academics beyond ourselves) work in higher education is serious and important work, in a serious and important work site – the academy. Yet, it is often felt by many an academic, particularly those within the education, arts and humanities fields, that the serious and important work that we do is negated by the technologies, in the Foucauldian sense, and apparatuses that operate in the academy which place high value on the scientific and empirical imperatives that have an imagined superworthiness bolstered by unrealistic measurabilities and unbending accountabilities. One need only to think of the pressures placed upon academics to publish in reified spaces and the consequential sense of failure if this is not achieved. The blunt-force effects of these imperatives are felt every day, and whilst we understand these may very well be the binds that tie us whilst in the academy, we also hold strongly to another set of values for our work and worth. These values do not detract from the seriousness of being accountable, transparent, outcome driven and competitive, and look to friendly (rather than cut-throat) considered scholarship. We imbue our work in values – within a set of guide ropes – that remind us of our humanness, rather than give ourselves over to cyborgian effect. And so in this spirit we commence with a play on words through naming our shared interests, not only as a coming *together*, but also *two-gather*. *Together* as known in normalised grammar conventions calls attention to our joining, but we are also signalling our warm-smile-on-the-face desire to transform conventions through a thoughtful playfulness with words, to rewrite our connection and therefore give breath to another grammar convention of coming *two-gather*. In reflecting on our practice, that is, what we have done and what we are aiming to do, our affinity with stories draws us close so that we *two-gather* to write this text.

DOI: 10.4324/9781315109190-1

## A love of stories

### *Tracey*

I grew up with the privilege of having a mother who was a storyteller, a good storyteller not only for the immediate family but also for the larger extended family. Her stories taught genealogy for learning about relationships, how to be with others of family and to know our own place within it. Her stories took me to places through telling about family and friends. Listening to her stories made you laugh, cry, be frightened, thoughtful, angry, sad, contemplative and satisfied. Telling stories was a very natural behaviour that taught, nurtured and prepared you for the future. Stories, I have come to appreciate, have been the lens through which I understand the world. There are many within my large family who are storytellers, finessed performers who can reduce a listener to tears from laughing or crying in equal measure. I continue to hold this love of stories close to me and contemplate that perhaps a contribution I have is the capacity to write stories and give back through this ability.

### *Louise*

I have savoured the world of stories since embarking on studies in early childhood education and forging a storytelling career from performing told stories as early childhood pedagogy, though the spark for stories was probably ignited much earlier. Like Tracey's mother, my mother too told stories, and still does today, of the happenings in her life. She especially loves the madness of life stories: those that make you chuckle at your own lunacy or delight at the wonderfully serendipitous. A yearning for stories has pervaded my adulthood, with this hunger somewhat satiated through active participation in storytelling guilds and festivals of the storytelling revival. Perhaps, as Berger and Quinney (2005) suggest,

> this revival reflects a culture that is ill at ease, that lacks compelling myths to bind us all together. Perhaps it has something to do with our sense of rootlessness, of separation from extended family . . . a way to resurrect something we never had.
>
> (pp. 8–9)

For more than 25 years, I have provided storytelling performances and workshops with young children at conferences, kindergartens, schools, museums, libraries and festivals. Through this passion for stories, I saw the great educative potential of storytelling early in my teaching career. I undertook an independent project on storytelling in education in the final year of my education degree, from which I published two articles (Phillips, 1999, 2010), which to my surprise continue to be searched for, read and cited. Once my twins were in kindergarten, I felt I had time to pursue a PhD into storytelling pedagogy from 2006 to 2010. The art of stories and storytelling are central to my world-view, and expressed through my practices as a professional storyteller, early childhood teacher, early childhood consultant and academic. I perform sto-ries, play with stories, write stories, present workshops on storytelling and weave stories and storytelling into research methodology and writings for their great capacity to cultivate deep understandings of what it means to live in this world. I draw my knowledge base of story and storytelling from more than 25 years of reading, writing and performing stories as a storyteller, being an active Storytellers' Guild member and researching story and storytelling.

From this shared love of stories, we now explain what we mean by story and storying.

We see *story* as the communication of what it means to be human, that tells of emplaced, relational tragedies, challenges and joys of living. Stories are spo-ken, gestured, danced, dramatised, painted, drawn, etched, sculpted, woven, stitched, filmed, written and any combination of these modes and more.

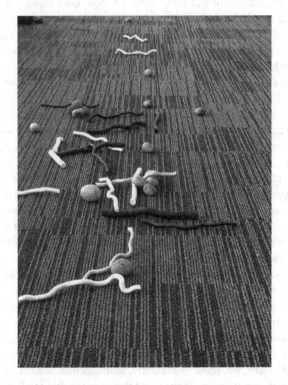

*Figure 1.1* Collectively storied sticks and stones from a storying workshop. Partici-pants were asked to recall a story that tells of who they are, imbue that story into a self-selected stone or stick and then place it into a collective composition.

Photograph taken by Louise.

*Story* is the word and approach that resonates for us, not *narrative*. Since at least the 1970s, there has been a narrative turn across a wide range of disciplines (e.g., theology, history, health, social sciences, business and therapy), though Sobol, Gentile and Sunwolf (2004) surmise that most of the scholars who have contributed to this turn would "only use the word storytelling in unguarded moments" (p. 2). They go on to explain that *narrative* is the term of choice for scholars with an interest "in appealing to the inclinations of adults in realms of power, prestige" (p. 2). We are more interested in all voices being heard, regardless of positionality (e.g., gender, race, class). We, like storytelling scholars Sobol, Gentile and Sunwolf, see an air of "pretension" and "over-intellectualization" in the term *narrative* (p. 2). We argue for the place of story in research, and we do so because it is everyday language used by people across cultures, ages, classes, disciplines and sectors.

For Tracey, *story* is the word her mob speaks. Indeed, apart from Aboriginal academic and creative circles, and even then, only some, the question to be asked is, "What is the use and value of the term *narrative* within Aboriginal spaces?" Do Aboriginal peoples say, "Come, sit, tell me a narrative?" Good go! The term *narrative* would be ridiculed and mocked as yet another white concept that has snuck its way in, to colonise, to reconfigure the freedoms inherent within Aboriginal talking spaces. Not to mention that there would be consequences for the bearer carrying this word *narrative* into the space – enough to say, in Aboriginal ways of knowing, "poor fella". *Poor fella* because the bearer has carried an unnecessary disruption to the Aboriginal space of telling stories. Nor do we want to position Aboriginal peoples as unknowing of the concept of narrative nor unknowing of how such concepts differentiate between those who have and those who have not – imagined superior intellectual currency because of the use of this language concept, narrative. Such simplistic binaries all too often permeate and trouble Aboriginal spaces, and work to trouble Aboriginal standpoint positions (Nakata, 2007). Unequivocally then, for Aboriginal peoples it is **story/ies**, not narrative.

For Louise, *story* is the word that makes her heart sing, that has bonded her in her work with children, storytellers and other artists. *Narrative* implies a specified genre structure, evoking didactic primary school English classes on how to write a narrative, whereas the invitation of "tell me a story" is a loose and open invitation to speak – to share your life happenings. The form doesn't matter; rather what matters is the lively retellings of connections to people and places. So, most importantly, embedded in our core social justice principles, we see *story* as the word that is accessible to all.

For story is not just written. Cherokee scholar Thomas King (2003) points out western assumptions that, to be complete, stories need to be written down, and that written literature has an inherent sophistication over oral stories, "that as we move from the cave to the condo we slough off the oral and leave it behind. Like an old skin" (p. 100). We argue to keep and treasure that skin, to decorate that skin, to add other layers to that skin.

We acknowledge the legacy of the work of narrative inquiry, though have not felt at home in that space, due to a disconnect with the term *narrative*. Key scholars of narrative inquiry Connelly and Clandinin (1990) distinguish the work that they do as researchers from the storied practices of the everyday and the everyday person:

> Narrative is both phenomenon and method. Narrative names the structured quality of experience to be studied, and it names the patterns of inquiry for its study. To preserve this distinction we use the reasonably well-established device of naming the phenomenon "story" and the inquiry "narrative".
>
> (p. 2)

We build on this distinction, and see storying as inquiry, as theorising, as sharing/presenting research. Narrative inquiry scholars have debated the term *narrative* (see Clandinin & Murphy, 2007), acknowledging a problem with the term in that it is often used as "a general meaning of any kind of prose" rather than "story form" (Polkinghorne interview with Clandinin & Murphy, 2007, p. 634). And Polkinghorne argues for the claiming of narrative research as that which is storied and follows story form, though without suggestion of substituting the term *narrative research* for *story/ing research*. We argue for storying research as research that is accessible by all, that is everyday practice, that crosses cultures, classes and modes: story and storying does that. The 2-year-old tells, listens to and asks for stories just as a 92-year-old does; a desert woman tells, listens to and asks for stories just as a corporate man does and so on. *Narrative* is not a word in common usage.

From the Aboriginal point of view, story, in all its Aboriginal-language terms, has always been.

From the white perspective, the word *story* emerged in English in the 1200s, derived from the Latin word *historia*, referring to an account of what had happened. The roots of story are embedded in the sharing of life's happenings (Smith, W., 2007). A distinction from the word *history* developed in the 1500s (Online etymology dictionary, 2017), which was very much based on a categorisation of history as truth and story as untruth/fiction. The age of enlightenment was most probably a catalyst for such a distinction, with its agenda of moral progress and reason, foregrounding truth. This was the time when new science emerged explaining the natural world as "an orderly domain governed by strict mathematical-dynamical laws," in which authority of knowledge was not claimed until subjected to rigorous sceptical questioning (Bristow, 2017). The legacy of such doubt, scepticism and lack of trust spawned a coldheartedness in western thinking that continues to determine what is truth and untruth, what is authorised knowledge and unauthorised knowledge. We see that stories do not seek to offer "totalizing truths", but instead provide "local situated truths" (Davies & Gannon, 2006, p. 4).

There are notes of privilege embedded in *narrative* and *history* that we reject and resist. One need only to look at the way in which dominant narratives of Aboriginal peoples in the Australian context are sutured into questionable facts of history that continue to hold sway (e.g., the history wars) (Macintyre, 2003). Neoliberalist realms of power were troubled by and questioned truth making in the field of history so much so that the white historian as ally, writing of Aboriginal massacres in Australian history, was brought under intense and prolonged interrogation. Polarised versions of the truth, constructed as either the black armband or the white blindfold, missed the total irony of white hysteria being played out in the absence of Aboriginal peoples' voices in the "debate". This situation confirmed what many Aboriginal people already know – the telling of our histories is primarily the prerogative of white people. Where do we find ourselves as Aboriginal people in Australian history – the victim, the vanquished, the sovereign warrior woman?

White archives document names, dates, places, roles, not stories – what is privileged and what is authorised. Archived facts and figures are labels for categories. Categorisation is an ongoing colonising practice (Smith, L. T., 2012). Stories tell of rich complexities, layered with symbolic meaning. Truth does not matter. Rather it is the gifting of new insights that matter. Historically, written records are dominated by those who could write and had status – typically upper class (gentry, royalty, seafarers, explorers), typically men and typically white – clearly a biassed perception of what is authorised knowledge. Telling stories is an oral tradition celebrated across cultures and classes, though we recognise, for varying cultural groups and for varying sensitivities, there are boundaries that cannot be crossed (we discuss this further in Chapter 3).

Other methodologies have emerged that foreground embodied lived experiences through story – such as writing-as-a-method-of-enquiry (Richardson, 1994), autoethnography (Ellis, 2004), performance ethnography (Alexander, 2005) and collective biography (Davies & Gannon, 2006) – to create an embodied understanding of phenomena. Arts-based research (see Leavy, 2014) offers a breadth of ways to work with story through visual, embodied and literary imagery. On the whole, these methodologies involve telling stories, listening to stories and writing stories to theoretically work through phenomena, truths and understandings. We recognise that many work with story ontologically, epistemologically and methodologically, and that many use the term *storying*. However, we have not located a text that specifically focuses on researching through, with and as storying, especially not one explored from by both Indigenous and non-Indigenous perspectives walking alongside each other. We have consequently composed this book as what we see as a necessary contribution to this space.

## Storying is . . .

We define *storying* as the act of making and remaking meaning through stories. The anthimeria (verbification) of *story* is purposeful to reflect that it is living and active rather than fixed, archived products. Stories are in constant unfolding. As Native American scholar Thomas King (2003) declares, "The truth about stories is that that's all we are" (p. 2). And Indian scholar Devika Chawla (2011) further explains,

> Stories breathe their own breaths, they are organic in nature, and dynamic in process. They are as primal to us as the organs in our body, and evolve as we do. We can control them to the extent that we choose the stories and the times we tell them. But even when we punctuate, reframe, retell or edit, we cannot but let them escape. As human beings, we are "storying" beings.
>
> (p. 16)

It is our position that stories are alive and in constant fluidity as we story with them. In research, we see storying as sitting and making emergent meaning with data slowly over time through stories. Connelly and Clandinin (1990) do use the words *storying* and *restorying*, as active meaning-making processes with story that both participants and researchers do. And they define *narrative inquiry* as "both a methodology and a way of understanding experience narratively" (Clandinin, 2013, p. 9) or "narrative ways of thinking about phenomena" (p. 11). Based on a Deweyan view of experience, narrative inquirers study lived experiences. We see storying as more than this. We see storying as what you do in the propositions/conceptualisations of research, in the gathering of data with others, in the theorising and analysis of data, in the presentation of research. Storying is axiological, ontological and epistemological. We argue for story as theory, as data, as process, as text on the ethical grounds of accessibility and foregrounding the marginalised.

For Aboriginal peoples, story and storytelling commenced at the beginning. Stories are embodied acts of intertextualised, transgenerational law and life spoken across and through time and place. In and of the everyday and everytime, stories – whether those that told of our origin or of our being now – all carry meaning: a theorised understanding that communicates the world. There are many storytellers within our communities and many stories are told. For white readers who would see this book as only pages that will give over to the badly named Dreaming stories of Aboriginal origins, they will be sadly disappointed. By not including stories of Aboriginal origin, there is not a dismissal of the value of such stories but rather, for Tracey, as the Aboriginal author, her speaking of stories and the sharing of other Aboriginal authored stories are those that are located firmly in the space and time when Aboriginal countries and peoples came to be colonised. Stories of the coloniser and Aboriginal ways of renegotiating Aboriginal being in colonised places, the ways in which Aboriginal people can recolonise country and how Aboriginal ways of knowing, being and doing (Martin, 2008; Arbon, 2008) in the contemporary everyday can be voiced and heard, are the focus in this book. In part, this focus reflects Tracey's own location as an Aboriginal person, one Aboriginal positionality in a sea of surviving colonising contexts. It is a location that respectfully acknowledges stories before white people came, and her writing about contemporary everyday storying weaves back, picking up the threads of age-old traditions and practices to tell different Aboriginal stories, speaking them into being. So, there is respect for the weft in the weave where stories are told by storytellers in Aboriginal country, where stories reach across and into other generations, where stories educate and entertain, where stories build the theoretical impulse for what we are naming as storying, through a differing lens, to firmly position our world views as Aboriginal peoples.

We now explain the centrality of storying in being human.

## Defining *the human* in storying

Humans are "storying" beings – and telling stories is a natural human habit (Gottschall, 2012). Stories cultivate a deeper sense of humanity (Arendt, 1958/1998; Bruner, 2003; Nussbaum, 1997). Story provides a way for humans to frame their understanding of the world, giving shape and order to it (Fisher, 1987). To Bruner, " 'great' storytelling is about compelling human plights that are accessible to 'readers'" (p. 35). We argue that stories aren't just for readers, but can also be spoken, danced, drawn, painted, filmed and so on. Bruner described how people suffering from the neurological condition of dysnarrativia (the inability to tell or understand stories) are unable to also sense what other people might be thinking, feeling or even seeing.

According to Bruner, these people present as having lost a sense of self as well as a sense of others. On this basis, Bruner concluded that we need the ability to tell and understand stories to develop an understanding of identity and humanity.

Attention to making meaning through story is ancient, as Clandinin and Rosiek (2007) acknowledge:

> Human beings have lived out and told stories about that living for as long as we could talk. And then we have talked about the stories we tell for almost as long. These lived and told stories and the talk about the stories are one of the ways that we fill our world with meaning and enlist one another's assistance in building lives and communities.
>
> (p. 35)

We argue that storying honours the legacy of our ancestors engaging in theorising and research from the emergence of language. We see research as a practice occurring across the world since the dawn of time, not only that which is "authorized" in western scholarship. Grand cultural stories, such as those referred to as myths, legends and folk tales (such naming we see as disagreeable, relegating stories to untruths), gift ontological and epistemological theories that are treasured by communities and passed on from generation to generation. Named in this way, stories as myths, legends and folk tales are left abandoned, set apart, positioned as lesser to the purities of evidentiary knowings, and rather are tainted by fanciful ways of being and telling, all confirmed in the deft articulation of those words antonymous with truth making. Consider the ways in which the historical Aboriginal subject was rendered childlike simultaneous to being barbarous. All this, whilst Aboriginal peoples were highly likely to be fluent in several languages, created environments that were disease free and lived in ontological knowledges that for thousands of generations practised peace for the land and the people. There are incommensurabilities. We hold that *truth* is a contested site. We are not simple folk who tell simple tales. We hold to a truth that stories and storying forms are created in sites of sophisticated knowledge, sites of higher knowledge.

Stories sustain cultures and languages. Louise's storytelling friend Wajuppa Tossa (2012) has for more than 20 years been telling Isan stories and training hundreds of others to tell Isan stories to sustain Isan language and culture in Thailand. Additionally, stories sustain Aboriginal Australian cultures, through story, song, dance and art.

In Aboriginal terms, sharing and connecting through stories with audiences draws on the traditions of responsibilities and reciprocities inherent in relationalities that tie back into kinship systems.

Across the globe, storytelling enables connection with the other. Even though storytellers may share a story that is not their personal experience, a good storyteller will always share something of herself through the intimacy of connection with her audience. This quality of storytelling Benjamin (1968/1999) describes as "traces of the storyteller [that] cling to the story the way the handprints of the potter cling to the clay vessel" (p. 91). In many ways, this personal sharing creates intimacy and thereby draws the listener in, as she identifies her life with that of the storyteller. There are points of connection that resonate with listeners, for they may have had similar experiences or they can imagine that the same could happen to them. This intimacy can invoke what Arendt (1958/1998) referred to as a web of human relationships, as the connection between storyteller, story and listener cultivates connections with others.

The relationship with others is at the core of storytelling and storying – there must be tellers and listeners. The fate and creation of the story depends on being with others, what Kristeva (2001) referred to as "inter-being" (p. 15). When Louise tells stories, those who she tells of are with her; she carefully holds their lived experiences in her hands and gently breathes life into them through embodied performative retelling. To Kristeva, the coimplication of selves and others is in the loop of storytelling. Storytelling implies an existence of community because it requires storytellers and audiences who listen and respond. The involvement of others is necessary for meaning. Benjamin (1968/1999), Arendt (1958/1998) and Kristeva all claim that in storytelling, meaning rests with the listeners. A story is a gift with layers of meaning to unwrap and sit with when, where and how required. "Storytelling reveals meaning without the error of defining it" (Arendt, 1970, p. 105). Meaning is thus never definitive, as listeners will create meanings applicable to their lives and experiences.

To Arendt (1958/1998), accounts of the actions people initiate tell more about the person than any tangible product produced by the person. We cherish Arendt's proposition that we can only know who somebody is by knowing the story in which she or he is the hero. In workshops where the authors have presented on storying, the audience has been invited to share the stories of who they are. The intimacy of these courageous stories readily evoke empathy, respect and "inter-being". Arendt explains the place of story in action through an examination of courage. "The connotation of courage . . . is in fact present in the willingness to act and speak at all, to insert oneself into the world and begin a story of one's own" (p. 186). Those who have the courage to start something new are heroes in their own stories. Such stories are theories; such stories astound and provoke ongoing tellings and thinking on what it means to be human and more-than-human.

We relish in the subjective world of storying, and are grateful to feminism for claiming and foregrounding subjectivity. Feminists argue for stories as central for understanding the lived experiences of gender, class and race oppression (Morley, 1997). For Aboriginal readers, a nod to feminism would place us on contentious ground. Certainly, white middle-class materialist forms of feminism have done little to elevate the agendas of black women and peoples globally. The creation of the term *womanist* by Alice Walker (1983) is a speaking back to these critiques, in which women of colour seek to include issues of class and race through a recognition of women's culture and power in an integrated world. Translated into the Australian context, womanist positions have their own particular Aboriginal-woman flavour that draws from traditions and practices of defining Aboriginal women's sovereign strength and power. It is a current practice of Aboriginal scholarship to speak into standpoint locations (Nakata, 2007; Moreton-Robinson, 2013), both as a way of naming oneself in Aboriginal epistemological practice, and of giving indirect acknowledgement to feminist theory as a source of standpoint methodology. By no means should women's – and especially Aboriginal women's – talkings back to white feminisms cease, for there remains many a power-sensitive dialogue (Haraway, 1988) to be spoken across the racialised, gendered and classed space of the Australian context. The Aboriginal standpoint methodology thus leans into feminist theory to acquire power sensitivity, not just internally to Aboriginal conversations, but especially in conversations between Aboriginal and non-Aboriginal peoples. In taking up this approach, Aboriginal peoples in many social spaces have made crucial contributions to critical understandings of colonising dimensions of power through storying of white institutional and ideological power (Arbon, 2008; Dodson, 2007; Dudgeon, 2010; Herbert, 2010; Gilbey, 2014). Circulating such knowledge can serve Indigenous purposes when fed carefully into trustworthy networks of wider reception. This book aims to be such a space.

Haraway (1991) offers further thought: "Feminists don't need a doctrine of objectivity that promises transcendence, a story that loses track of its mediations just where someone might be held responsible for something, and unlimited instrumental power" (p. 187). She continues that feminists

> don't want to theorise the world, much less act within it, in terms of Global systems, but we do need an earth-wide network of connections, including the ability partially to translate knowledges among very different – power-differentiated – communities. We need the power of modern critical theories of how meanings and bodies get made, not in order to deny meaning and bodies, but in order to live in meanings and bodies that have a chance for a future.

(p. 187)

We see stories and storying translating embodied knowledges from diverse communities who are often silenced or their voices rarely given airplay. For these reasons, we speak back to positivist hierarchical arrogant privileging of what counts as knowledge, because "the doctrines of objectivity . . . threatened our [feminist] sense of collective historical subjectivity and agency and our 'embodied' accounts of the truth" (p. 186). As Celtic mythologist Sharon Blackie (2016) points out, "Women were always the story-givers, the memory-keepers, the dreamers" (p. 361).

Through storying we foreground bodies (privileging sensation, emotion and spirit) and relationships – an antithesis to much of the modern academic joint, which is designed and still operates on Cartesian thinking of separating the mind from the mechanical pragmatics of the body. In Aboriginal storying, carriage of emotion, relatedness and spirituality brings Aboriginal life essence, logic and ethic to storying. It is central to Aboriginal standpoint positioning. How well the body and the mind work together is the measure of the good storyteller, though we acknowledge there are few spaces in the academy where the storyteller can be. The privileging of the mind in academia has been read in Jungian terms by Sobol et al. (2004), who found that

> the Academy has evolved in a patriarchal environment dedicated to the principle of Logos, the domain of rationality, knowledge, and abstraction. Storytelling embraces the feminine principle of Eros, which carries emotion, relatedness, and spirituality; and that Eros principle has shaped the environment and the orientation of storytelling devotees and their gatherings.
>
> (p. 5)

The mind is privileged in the academy for its production of causal explanations, whilst sensation is often deemed as a source of untruth and illusions or of inconsequential value. Individualism and objectivity are honoured. Such is enacted through individual offices (solitude for the mind), bodies only used to get the mind from one meeting place to another, and being tracked individually according to their individual outputs and individual national and international recognition. We also recognise that these measures privilege white patriarchal norms, and critical Aboriginal embodiments (perhaps the most obvious contrast to white patriarchy in the academy), wanting to story research whilst being tangled up in these norms, face challenges to standpoint positions which talk country, talk family, talk stories as theory. Stories have hearts and souls – they breathe – they are alive (Frank, 2010). Hence, we use the anthimeria *storying* to infer an ongoing creating and meaning-making process. And that by working with bodies, sensation, feelings and relationships we argue that there is capacity to bring more inclusive and accessible understanding and insight into research.

## Together/two-gather

In sum, our strong intent is to be situated with story, and through its verbification of *storying* we celebrate its living state. Through critical theories, we assert storying over knowledge produced in the name of narrative. We see that story, stories and storying belong to all. Our positioning commences with a critical framing of storying to push back onto questions of what counts as truth. For us, this mode of research produces creative, thoughtful and felt spaces that provoke deep, resonant thought to the human and more-than-human project. From this platform, we now move to share how we are emplaced – our roots – our located positionality through ancestral storying that we two have gathered as re-presentation of the humanness of our work.

## References

*Aboriginal Protection and Restriction of the Sale of Opium Act 1897* (Qld). Retrieved from www.foundingdocs.gov.au/resources/transcripts/qld5_doc_1897.pdf

Alexander, B. (2005). Performance ethnography: The reenacting and inciting of culture. In N. Denzin & Y. Lincoln (Eds.), *The Sage handbook of qualitative research* (pp. 411–441). Thousand Oaks, CA: Sage.

Anderson, B. (1983). *Imagined communities: Reflections on the origin and spread of nationalism* (2nd ed.). London: Verso.

Arbon, V. (2008). *Arlathirnda Ngurkarnda Ityirnda: Being-knowing: Doing-decolonising indigenous tertiary education.* Brisbane: Post Pressed.

Arendt, H. (1998). *The human condition* (2nd ed.). Chicago: The University of Chicago Press (Original work published 1958).

Benjamin, W. (1999). *Illuminations* (H. Zorn, Trans.). London: Pimlico (Original English version published 1968).

Berger, R. J., & Quinney, R. (2005). The narrative turn in social inquiry. In R. J. Berger & R. Quinney (Eds.), *Storytelling sociology: Narrative as social inquiry* (pp. 1–11). Boulder, CO: Lynne Rienner Publishers.

Blackie, S. (2016). *If women rose rooted: The journey to authenticity and belonging.* London: September Publishing.

Bourdieu, P. (1986). The forms of capital. In J. Richardson (Ed.), *Handbook of theory and research for the sociology of education* (pp. 241–258). New York: Greenwood Press.

Bristow, W. (2017, Summer). *Enlightenment: The Stanford encyclopedia of philosophy.* Retrieved from https://plato.stanford.edu/entries/enlightenment/

Bruner, J. (2003). Self-making narratives. In R. Fivusch & C. A. Haden (Eds.), *Auto-biographical memory and construction of a narrative self: Developmental and cultural perspectives* (pp. 209–225). Mahwah, NJ: Lawrence Erlbaum Associates.

Bunda, T. (2014). *The relationship between indigenous peoples and the university: Solid or what!* (Doctoral thesis). University of South Australia, Australia.

Chawla, D. (2011). Between stories and theories: Embodiments, disembodiments, and other struggles. In D. Chawla & A. Rodriguez (Eds.), *Liminal traces: Storying, performing, and embodying postcoloniality* (pp. 13–24). Rotterdam, The Netherlands: Sense Publishers.

Clandinin, D. J. (2013). *Engaging in narrative inquiry*. Walnut Creek, CA: Left Coast Press.

Clandinin, D. J., & Murphy, M. S. (2007). Looking ahead: Conversations with Elliot Mishler, Don Polkinghorne, & Amia Lieblich. In D. J. Clandinin (Ed.), *Handbook of narrative inquiry: Mapping a methodology* (pp. 632–651). Thousand Oaks: Sage.

Clandinin, D. J., & Rosiek, J. (2007). Mapping a landscape of narrative inquiry: Borderland spaces and tensions. In D. J. Clandinin (Ed.), *Handbook of narrative inquiry: Mapping a methodology* (pp. 35–76). Thousand Oaks: Sage.

Connelly, F. M., & Clandinin, D. J. (1990). Stories of experience and narrative inquiry. *Educational Researcher, 19*(5), 2–14.

Davies, B., & Gannon, S. (2006). *Doing collective biography*. Berkshire: Open University Press.

Dodson, P. (2007). Whatever happened to reconciliation? In J. Altman & M. Hinkson (Eds.), *Coercive reconciliation: Stabilise, normalise exit Aboriginal Australia* (pp. 21–30). North Carlton, Australia: Arena Publications Association.

Dudgeon, P., Kelley, K., & Walker, R. (2010). Closing the gaps in and through indigenous health research: Guidelines, processes and practices. *Australian Aboriginal Studies, 2*, 81–91.

Ellis, C. (2004). *The ethnographic I: A methodological novel about autoethnography*. Walnut Creek, CA: Altamira Press.

Fisher, W. R. (1987). *Human communication as narration*. Columbia: University of South Carolina Press.

Frank, A. W. (2010). *Letting stories breathe: A socio-narratology*. Chicago: University of Chicago Press.

Gilbey, K. (2014). *Privileging First Nations knowledge: Looking back to move forward* (Doctoral thesis). Batchelor Institute of Indigenous Tertiary Education, Australia.

Gottschall, J. (2012). *The storytelling animal: How stories make us human*. Boston: Houghton Mifflin Harcourt.

Haraway, D. (1988). Situated knowledges: The science question in feminism and the privilege of partial perspective. *Feminist Studies, 14*(3), 574–599.

Haraway, D. (1991). *Simians, cyborgs, and women*. New York: Routledge.

Herbert, J. (2010). Indigenous studies: Tool of empowerment within the academe. *Australian Journal of Indigenous Education, 39*, 22–31.

King, T. (2003). *The truth about stories: A native narrative.* Minneapolis: University of Minnesota Press.

Kristeva, J. (2001). *Hannah Arendt: Life is a narrative* (R. Guberman, Trans.). New York: Columbia University Press.

Leavy, P. (2014). *Method meets art: Arts-based research practice.* New York: Guildford Publications.

Martin, K. L. (2008). *Please knock before you enter: Aboriginal regulation of outsiders and the implications for researchers.* Teneriffe: Post Pressed.

McIntrye, S., & Clark, A. (2003). *The history wars.* Carlton, Victoria: Melbourne University Press.

Moreton-Robinson, A. (2013). Towards an Australian indigenous women's standpoint theory: A methodological tool. *Australian Feminist Studies, 28*(78), 331–347.

Morley, L. (1997). A class of one's own: Women, social class and the academy. In P. Mahony & C. Zmroczek (Eds.), *Class matters: Working-class women's perspectives on social class* (pp. 109–122). London: Taylor and Francis.

Nakata, M. (2007). *Disciplining the savages: Savaging the discipline.* Canberra: Aboriginal Studies Press.

Native Names. (1898, December 17). *Evening news (Sydney, NSW: 1869–1931),* p. 8 (EVENING NEWS CHRISTMAS NUMBER). Retrieved from http://nla. gov.au/nla.news-article114041354

Nussbaum, M. (1997). *Cultivating humanity: A classical defense of reform in liberal education.* Cambridge, MA: Harvard University Press.

Online Etymology Dictionary. (2017). *Story.* Retrieved from www.etymonline.com/ index.php?term=story

Phillips, L. G. (1999). The role of storytelling in early literacy development. *Rattler, 51,* 12–15.

Phillips, L. G. (2010). *Young children's active citizenship: Storytelling, stories and social actions* (Doctoral thesis). Queensland University of Technology, Australia.

Richardson, L. (1994). Writing: A method of inquiry. In N. K. Denzin & Y. S. Lincoln (Eds.), *Handbook of qualitative research* (pp. 516–529). Thousand Oaks, CA: Sage.

Said, E. (1978). *Orientalism.* New York: Pantheon Books.

Schamberger, K. (2006). *150 years of the NSW registry of births, deaths and marriages.* Retrieved from www.australianhistoryresearch.info/150-years-of-the-nsw-registry-of-births-deaths-and-marriages/

Smith, L. T. (2012). *Decolonising methodologies: Research and indigenous peoples* (2nd ed.). London: Zed Books.

Smith, W. (2007). *Origin of the word 'story'.* Retrieved from www.waitsel.com/ screenwriting/Story.html

Sobol, J., Gentile, J., & Sunwolf. (2004). Once upon a time: An introduction to the inaugural issue. *Storytelling, Self, Society: An Interdisciplinary Journal of Storytelling Studies, 1*(1), 1–7.

Tossa, W. (2012). Global storytelling and local cultural preservation and revitalization. *Storytelling, Self, Society, 8*(3), 194–201.

Trask, H.-K. (1993). *From a native daughter: Colonialism and sovereignty in Hawai'i.* Honolulu: University of Hawaii Press.

Walker, A. (1983). *In search of our mothers' gardens: Womanist prose.* San Diego: Harcourt Brace Jovanovich.

White, J. (Ed.). (2016). *Permission: The international interdisciplinary impact of Laurel Richardson's work.* Innovations and Controversies: Interrogating Educational, Change, 4. Rotterdam, The Netherlands: Sense Publishers.

# 2 Locating self in place and ancestral storying

To commence our contribution to storying, we locate ourselves – who are we in the human project, locating our roots to story our cultural identities. We share ancestral stories gathered and held in our whole of beings as part of our lifelong identity work. We feel the roots of each other's stories, historical pulses and pains, drawing threads and knots and tensions between stories.

## The basket

*Tracey*

In a previous life, somewhere between teaching in the classroom and working in the university, I was employed in the Aboriginal and Torres Strait Islander Branch of the Queensland Education Department. Part of my role was to assess the quality of resources that would support the teaching of Aboriginal and Torres Strait Islander studies in the school curriculum. I recall a film resource which showed basket-making skills used by Aboriginal women in the north of Queensland. I set about, with imperfect remembering, making this basket.

I am fascinated and perplexed by the gardening-design uptake of palm trees where I live. I think these plants belong in the tropical north. Regardless, palm trees are an established feature in modern urban design and, with the generosity of the westerly wind and my neighbour's palm trees, a palm frond was delivered into my backyard.

To create the basic rectangular pattern for the basket, I first sawed off the stem and frond. What is left is the sheath, that part which wraps around the trunk of the palm tree. The sheath is hard and unforgiving, so in order to work with this stiff fibrous material it needs to be made malleable by being wet. I submerged the sheath in my bathtub, weighed down by a cast-iron

DOI: 10.4324/9781315109190-2

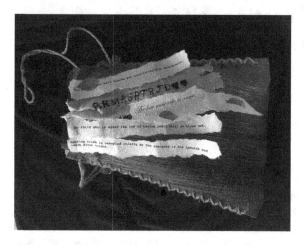

*Figure 2.1* Basket of entangled archives.
Photograph taken by Louise.

pot so that it could be thoroughly soaked. (The cast-iron pot left an imprint in the fibre, and though I was initially disappointed, my colleague Robyn, an academic artist, saw the stain of the pot as a value added to the design. Blessed be artists for seeing the world differently.) After a few days, I took the sheath from the water. At the longest edges, I folded the sheath inwards about 2 cm to make a seam. I then folded the sheath almost exactly in half. One half was longer by approximately 5–6 cm. Along the edges of the basket I punched holes with a nail at equidistance so that I could stitch the edges together. For this, I used jute in a cross-stitch pattern. I added some decoration to the basket by sewing in the eucalyptus nuts which I had painted and threaded with jute. I plaited a jute strap for carrying the basket (the strap is placed around your forehead like a headband and when carried in this way allows the basket to nestle on your back between your shoulder blades whilst your hands are free for gathering) and its other function was for hanging the basket. The finished basket was oiled, which I am hoping helps in the preservation and mimics the transfer of body oil from person to basket, if it were a basket in use at the time of BC (before Cook).

The photograph shows a series of words and phrases coming to lay across the fibrous front of the basket. These phrases and words are taken directly from our archival research initiated, in part, from those stories told to us by family of our ancestral roots, and holding that knowledge and reclaiming that knowledge through women's crafts, of needle penetrating fibre to (re)present. The basket and archival documents meld to present our story-ing research, moving through time and place to dig deeper, to critically examine and to imagine lives. There is a cathartic effect, as hooks (1995) notes, "to tell one's story and the process of telling is symbolically a gesture of longing to recover the past in such a way that one experiences both a sense of reunion and a sense of release" (p. 158). When storying is organic, embodied – through seeing, hearing and feeling, in becoming and known, recited, remembered and recalled – emergent conditions coalesce, to form in thought, to speak anew the colonial texts that would make our ancestors disembodied, as if separate from the times and ideologies that would place them as less than human. We restory their lives, by tearing up the archival scripts, drawing from our theoretical baskets, imagining a differing human-ity for those from which we come. Stories theorised for our heads, stories stitched into our hearts. As Blaze Kwaymullina (2007) notes,

> Stories spoken from the heart hold a transformational power, they are a way for one heart to speak to another. They are a means for sharing knowledge, experience and emotion. A story spoken from the heart can pierce you, become a part of you and change the way you see yourself and the world. Listening to a heart story is a way of showing respect, a silent acknowledgement of what the speaker has lived through and where they have come from. Stories can also transform the speaker. Sharing the past can ease old pains, soothe deep hurts and remind you of old joys, hopes and dreams.
>
> (p. 6)

## Naming ourselves

### *Tracey*

Story is the tool through which I investigate identity work. Knowing who I am and where I come from is but part of my identification. It is equally important to know that my individual identity is very much bound up with others, which includes family and other relations. I tell a story of my pater-nal grandmother and father.

The realities of being named with an Aboriginal identity in colony Aus-tralia is not without contention. I purposefully couple colony and Australia and in doing so borrow from Haunani-Kay Trask (1993), Hawaiian warrior woman and scholar, as a reminder that acts of colonisation have persistent effects on the lives of Aboriginal peoples. One of these effects is for the dominant to determine the ways in which we are named. I acknowledge that within Aboriginal communities there is an unsettling about the naming of us, be it as Indigenous Australian or Aboriginal peoples. Part of this unsettling rejects the term *Indigenous*, which became popularised through government stylus. I often wonder whether this was as a result of white public servants' fingers become tired and annoyed at typing "Aboriginal and Torres Strait Islander". Yet, in taking up the term *Aboriginal* we need to be reminded that this word too is not of our own making; it is a colonial construct. There were no Aboriginal people before white people. Langton (1993) reminds us, "before contact there were Yolngu, Pitjantjatjara, Walpiri, Waka Waka . . . and so on" (p. 32). I have childhood rememberings of my father naming himself as Wakka Wakka and proudly so. In generic terms, we spoke of ourselves and others as Gooris. To speak in this way is part of my family's language of identification. Naming ourselves makes us human.

In 1998, I received a Queensland Department of Environment grant to undertake family history. And though I had oral family stories, I wanted to investigate further about the Purga Mission and the Barambah/Cherbourg Aboriginal Reserve because of the connectedness of these institutions to my larger family. Many of the older Aboriginal families within Ipswich have the same connections. My intention was to develop a fuller history, coupling the oral and archival with genealogies which I would record, for my families, for the other Aboriginal families and for future generations. This research was important for me. It would allow me and other Aboriginal peoples to speak back to dominant white practices that worked to erase our being through stealing our generations and dispossessing us of our lands, thus leaving many within our communities without a complete genealogy to recite and therefore an incapacity to know all of our family and to know in deep ways our country. Through this project I had wanted to tell stories of resistance, survival, the tragic, the celebratory and the comical.

It was an interesting project that took me on my first venture into the state archives. For Aboriginal peoples yet to enter the archives, be prepared. In one respect, there is a sense of benevolence, a gratefulness that the colonisers were so, in Aboriginal ways of talking, corked up, to record so much detail yet, at the same time, a sense of being astounded that the colonisers were so corked up to record so much detail. Here, the detail was not about naming Aboriginal peoples as human.

I digress for a moment. In my doctoral study I named the university as a white institution complicit in the colonial project and did so to theoretically argue the ways in which white institutional and ideological power colonises knowledge production. I wrote,

> The colonial knowing of us as objects of study travelled from the diaries of white "explorers", the records of government officials, the observations of squatters and colonial news print, coalesced into "scientific"

notes in the field and travelled further to laboratories, lecture theatres and research proposals in anthropology and archaeology departments at universities. In this way the university retained a complementary arrangement with the colonial project. The colonial project initially engaged in the dispossession of Aboriginal peoples from our lands. The university initially engaged in knowing Aboriginal peoples from the perspective of white people: a dispossessing of ourselves from ourselves.

(Bunda, 2014, p. 116)

From the time of this project and researching in the archives I have a copy of a document, an Aboriginal census for June 1928 of the Barambah Settlement, Murgon, Queensland. The interconnectedness between this census document and the institution of the university is plainly stated. It was compiled by an accountant for the Barambah Settlement (possibly an administrator for the Chief Protector of Aborigines) and, interestingly, the other contributors named their location as the University of Sydney. Did these University of Sydney contributors know they were assisting in the dispossessing of ourselves from ourselves? Probably not. For as much as the census is constituted by labels that name in particularly ways, there is a derogation of Aboriginal peoples, labels interpolating with senses of dehumanisation. Invisible stitching that would keep the interface, between black and white, firm and secure. Neat, controlled, all stitched up.

The census went into great detail in classifying Aboriginality and in the absence of critical consciousness was framed in a historical time whereby Aboriginal peoples were captured under the Act (Aboriginal Protection and Restriction of the Sale of Opium Act, 1897):

The census is divided into eight subsections as follows:

1   Full blood adult males.
2   Full blood adult females.
3   Full blood male children.
4   Full blood female children.
5   Caste adult males.
6   Caste adult females.
7   Caste male children.
8   Caste female children.

The classificatory system went further:

In sections 5–6–7 and 8 the caste of each individual has been recorded. The fraction indicates the full blood aboriginal percentage and the succeeding letter or letters indicate the nature of the caste.

C indicates Chinese blood
W "European"
N "Negroid"
K "Melanesian" or Polynesian blood.

Thus ½ C indicates a hybrid between a full blood aborigine and a Chinaman and ½ WK indicates an individual one of whose parents was a full blood aborigine while the other was a half caste Kanaka.

Racial hierarchical systems were firmly imprinted in this classificatory system.

The document identified that

All individuals in sections 3–4–7 and 8 are 14 years of age or younger.

My father did not have a birth certificate. This was made known when he applied to enlist for World War II. His year and date of birth were orally recorded by an accidental meeting of my two grandmothers who crossed paths at the Department of Native Affairs where they were each seeking permissions to travel. Movements of Aboriginal people were vigorously policed under the Act, ensuring that no unwarranted Aboriginal presences would cross the boundaries between black and white and thus avert imagined threatenings of safety and security for white people. Such imagined threats and the control of Aboriginal movements were recast as a need "to protect" Aboriginal people from the vices of white societies. In turn this signalled the segregation of Aboriginal peoples away from the wider community onto Aboriginal Reserves – designated by the white nation as spaces of protection. Though, depending on the mental state of the "supervisors" in care of Aboriginal peoples, such reserves could, in fact, be punitive spaces where heartbreaking sadness, terror, hunger and deprivation reigned. Standing in the offices of the Department of Native Affairs my maternal grandmother was pregnant with my mother and my paternal grandmother held the hand of a little boy, about 2 years of age. This is how verification of my father's birthday came to be known, and it is this verification, relayed back to the Department of Native Affairs by my father, that enabled him to secure an "official" authorisation that stood in the absence of a birth certificate, making way for his enlistment.

I come back round to the story of the census document. A Vincent Bunder was identified as ½ W followed by the number 6, the age of the child. Is this my father? Based on the knowings of my grandmothers, my father would have been born in 1921, and at the time and date of this census he would have been 6, for his birthday is not until September, though the spelling of our surname is not correct. He is identified as a half caste with his father being a white man.

Regimes of dispossessing ourselves from ourselves were well established on the reserves and missions through regimented control, minimalist and poor-quality education and systems of slavery that ensured Aboriginal people lived up to the racialised standard of being indolent. The sale of my grandmother's labour was a contracted agreement between white men, those who sold and those who bought. On the Queensland colonial frontier, black women sweated their labour – cooking, cleaning, washing, ironing, caring for children, feeding, herding the animals, fencing and much more. Under this regime, my father was born. Was he born of love or violence? I will never know.

This racialised language, this system of classifying, had indelible, long-lasting effect on the ways of being for Aboriginal peoples. Sadly, the language of full blood, half caste and quarter caste stayed within our families and communities. Within the white communities, this racialised language remained the language of supremacy for exerting power over our Aboriginal being. My light brown–coloured skin, like my father's, set us apart from the rest of our darker-coloured family members. Whilst there was safety in being physically different in my family, this was not the case when I did not have the protection of my family. As a child, when I crossed over into white spaces, my Aboriginality would sometimes come to be a point of fascination and sometimes fetishsisation. Sometimes people were confronting to the point of violent. I remember being questioned as to the blood quantum of my Aboriginality to verify my authenticity as an Aboriginal person to the white people who asked the question. Was I half caste? Was I quarter caste? These labels were commonly used in dialogues from hurtful and hateful white peoples to many an Aboriginal person. As long as I live I will despise these labels. A politics of pigmentation, a foul vapour would come to lie on my skin in these moments, to remind me that I was less than Aboriginal, less than white, something in between – possibly a freak.

In my family, the most influential discourse was born of the intellectual warriorship from both my mother and father. The meeting of the maternal salt water and the paternal fresh water sovereignties, epistemologies and pedagogies fed my standpoint (Haraway, 1991), and it has taught me to know, look and speak in particular ways to rebut dominant and subjugating ways of knowing us as Aboriginal peoples. This legacy informs the theories in my basket, a critical accessory for my work in the white institution of education (Bunda, 2014). Colonial ideological effects continue to permeate white institutions, albeit in new forms. A failure to remain vigilant to these effects places Aboriginal people in unsafe and insensitive spaces, ironically in our own country where our sovereignties should be acknowledged and

respected. The messy exhaustive work of combat-deflecting insult, preju-
dice, stereotypes and racism detracts from the liberatory work of decolonisation and recolonisation. As researchers, storying ourselves in this country
names a fundamental step in making ourselves human.

## *Louise*

Hearing Tracey's story of naming self further prickles the troubling of being
a white Australian. I feel shame for the pain and suffering my storying sister
and her family have suffered at the hands of white colonisation. The troubling of naming myself as Australian first stirred when I travelled around
India in 1987 for 3 months at age 18 (prior to this I grew up in a relatively
sheltered life in a middle-class suburb, second youngest of seven). Each time
I met someone in India I was commonly asked, "Where you from?" and after
my reply, "Australia", I was met with the uncomfortable stereotypes of beer-
guzzling, sport-loving men. And as I answered, I wondered more and more
what that meant. I did (and still do) not feel proud to answer "Australia". I
knew I needed to dig deeper to understand the shaping of Australia and what
it meant to be a white Australian. With Australia being "a relatively newly
formed nation" built on colonisation, a declaration of Australian citizenship
does not reveal ethnic heritage, nor does it enact the honest critical reflection
required in the naming of ourselves to make us human that Tracey illustrated.
As Nicolacopoulos and Vassilacopoulos (2014) explain, "As unloved and
non-loving the colonial subject hides the depth of his or her ontological emptiness by engaging in criminal activity the world over" (p. 45). I can see how
the rise of scepticism and reduced trust in the age of enlightenment has fed
the hardened state of the colonial subject who perpetuates self/other directed
violence. Naming self as Australian is riddled with "ontological emptiness".
I descend from displaced ancestors – diaspora – though there is little honesty
in the heritage and territorial claim of the white Australian.

In my return from India, I searched for stories of the colonisation of Australia. Not the white stories; I had enough of those in school – year after
year the same white "facts" repeated, a whitewashed version of history. I
first went to my local library and found *Massacres to Mining: The Colonisation of Australia* by Janine Roberts (1981). I was nauseatingly sickened;
a deep-seated unsettling penetrated my whole being. Janine Roberts awak-
ened me to the sheer terror Aboriginal Peoples have been (and continue to
be) subjected to since colonisation. I became unsettled, aware that my kin
were overstaying visitors on stolen land. I was/am ashamed of the incessant
violation. There was/is nothing to be proud of in the making of the nation
Australia. As Henry Reynold's (1999) well-known book later asked, *Why
Weren't We Told?*

And so I searched for kith and kin – as to who my ancestors were, where they came from and what my ancestors' roles and experiences were in the horrors of genocide under the sinister mask of nation building. As Nicola-copoulos and Vassilacopoulos (2014) point out, without a self-conscious white-Australia philosophy, we have yet to formulate an answer to "Where do you come from?" This question demands "white Australians to respond by situating ourselves philosophically in relation to our origins . . . as the only thing that is our very own" (p. 15). Origins only offer some answers to our out-of-placeness (*atopos*). What Nicolacopoulos and Vassilacopoulos then argue is that what white Australians need to face is the naming of our relations to the spaces we inhabit.

I searched my family history – back three to five generations along all lineages to arrivals in Australia, to locate cultural origins and to see what role my ancestors played in the colonisation project – to see my ancestors' relations to the forming of colony Australia. Much of this was hidden by the white practice of "sweeping under the carpet" past shames – "bodies turn away from the others who witness the shame" (Ahmed, 2005, p. 75).

Across decades of searching, all I have found is the appropriation of Aboriginal-language names to property. My mother's mother's mother's father's parents (Samuel and Maryann Markwell) owned and managed a farming property that was named Mungaree (Yugara language for "place of fishes" in 1865 in the area that is now known as Slack's Creek, one of the first settled areas in the region now covered by Logan City Council of Bris-bane) (Keirs, 1997). My great-great-grandparents were the second owners of Mungaree after John Slack (Logan City Council, 2017). I could locate no trace of the Markwell's relationship with local Yugara people, nor how John Slack came to name the property Mungaree. My father also appropriated an Aboriginal-language name to our family home. He grew up on Kulgoa Ave-nue in Ryde, and so decided to get the word *Kulgoa* painted on metal letters adhered to the front of our house, to the left of our front door. We were never told what it meant, but just accepted it as the name of our house. Ryde his-tory of street names states *kulgoa* means "running through", though no lan-guage group is identified. On 17 December 1898, the *Sydney Evening News* on p. 8 had an article titled "Native Names and Their Meanings", which lists the meaning of dozens of Aboriginal-language words, including *kulgoa*. A continuing thread the unnamed author sustains throughout the article is how pretty sounding these names are compared to the English names given to many places, such as Dead Dog Beach and Mount Misery.

And so I wonder, was permission ever sought to use *Mungaree* and *Kul-goa* to brand property? I imagine John Slack asked Yugara people, "What do you call this place?" And perhaps he somehow felt better for claiming the land as his own by using the local people's name for it. In the comfort of their whiteness, my ancestors saw Australia's First Nations' people as a group that could provide "pretty" names. There seemed no interest beyond this, nor horror at the violent atrocities to Aboriginal peoples that were happening around them. Perhaps they felt worlds apart. After all, the governing bodies did all they could to keep Aboriginal people away from white occupiers. The theft and appropriation of Aboriginal language illustrates a tokenistic naming of my ancestors' relations to their inhabitation of Australian country and reeks of the mindset of western liberal property ownership. And that property ownership is an imperative of whiteness, though to authentically confront our relations with the inhabitation of Australian country, Nicolacopoulos and Vassilacopoulos (2014) propose that we confront the question of ownership of Australian territory – that we declare that Australia has been built on the lying premise of *terra nullius*.

The secret instructions that were given to Captain James Cook in 1768 by the Commissioners for Executing the Office of Lord High Admiral of Great Britain, before he set sail to observe the transit of Venus in the Pacific, were to map and observe the eastern coast of the land then known as New Holland:

> You are also with the Consent of the natives to take possession of Convenient Situations in the Country in the Name of the King of Great Britain; or, if you find the Country uninhabited take possession for His Majesty by setting up proper marks and inscriptions, as first discoverers and possessors.
>
> (Beaglehole, 1955, p. cclxxxii)

In the journals of Cook's journey up the east coast, they noted frequent sightings of numerous Aboriginal peoples and frequent attempts to meet that were repelled. Cook then disregarded all the evidence of inhabitation that he witnessed first-hand and, when he and his crew reached the top of the eastern coast, he planted the British flag on a small island in the Torres Strait (named through this act as Possession Island) and claimed possession of the entire eastern coast for Britain (Beaglehole, 1955; see Gordon Bennett's storying through painting of this act in *Possession Island* [1991], www.ngv.vic.gov.au/gordonbennett/education/04.html). Joseph Banks, the botanist who accompanied Cook's journey, was later instrumental in pushing for what became named by Britain as New South Wales as a penal settlement at the Beauchamp Committee on Transportation in 1785. Banks argued that no purchasing of land would be required (as was the case with the other contenders Africa, Canada and the West Indies), as the Aboriginal people showed no interest in what Captain Cook and his crew had to offer

(Renwick, 1991). The perceptions, decisions and actions of these two men have created monumental devastation through widespread displacement and genocide for millions of people, all flora and fauna, land and water of what are now known in English as Australian territories. Such unconscionable arrogance, that Cook and Bank felt that their perception of other people's lived practice was the authority to determine that their existence and inhabitation was of insignificance. "Ontological emptiness . . . the colonial subject then enacts violence against all others whose acts of solidarity serve as the perpetual ground for the repetition of this self/other directed violence" (Nicolacopoulos & Vassilacopoulos, 2014, p. 45).

The absence of any archived encounters between my ancestors and local Aboriginal peoples speaks volumes as to whose history is privileged. White middle- and upper-class histories are documented and archived. My parents did share with me ancestral names, places and brief titbits of life events sprinkled throughout my growing up, and I asked more questions in my adulthood, and searched through archives finding much, much more. My mother also acquired two self-published family history books from her mother's lineage. In the ancestral-searching conversations that Tracey I shared in preparation for this book, white privilege in archives became more and more visible. I could readily search grave records back five generations, yet grave records of Aboriginal communities such as for Tracey's grandmother proved elusive. Aboriginal protection and welfare boards recorded Aboriginal births, deaths and marriages of people who were defined as "Aborigines" and "supervised" by the board, and church bodies managing missions also kept records (Australian Institute of Aboriginal and Torres Strait Islander Studies, 2017). The extensive records that were kept were an abhorrent invasion of privacy and abusive scientific categorisation, such as the dehumanising practice of listing Tracey's father as "½ W 6". These records aren't readily available via the Internet. Instead, permission has to be sought to access the records through state and national archives. Private genealogy companies (such as ancestry. com) are designed for white middle-class ancestries. Archives categorise and control and privilege a scientific voice. They track, categorise and surveil. I feel for the lostness of incomplete genealogies, through absence of intergenerational sharing of emplaced, embodied stories.

## *Grand*mothering stories

We look to our grandmother's and great-grandmother's stories to connect womanhood across time, culture and place, through storying archives and family stories. By doing this we create and hold women's time which, as Julia Kristeva (1981) describes, is "extra subjective time, cosmic time, occasional vertiginous visions and unnameable jouissance" (p. 16). Like Nye, Barker and Charteris (2016), by looking to ancestral maternal stories we locate, embody and embrace displacement, loss, hardship, survival and care across generations as a valid means for "new cartographies for research" (p. 189). The flesh we have crafted and woven into stories to bring archives to life translates historical evidence offering generative meaning making (Radstone, 2010) to reveal lineage and emplace our intergenerational positionality. The concerns of contestable history and academic rigour (i.e., what is truth and whose truth is authorised) are not welcome or relevant here.

### *Tracey*

The other story that I wish to share is that of my patrilineal grandmother, the one who held the hand of my father as they waited in the Department of Native Affairs for permission to travel.

I did not know this grandmother; my older brothers knew her best for she had passed before I was born. So I know her through the stories of my father and mother, and from having dug into the archives I know her from the writings of "protectors" and government administrators as just another "Aborigine", as a functional statement on a page, a fragment of a broken-up story that was reflective of Aboriginal peoples of the times. There are a few of her own handwritten letters.

I can remember searching in the archives, documents strewn across the desk, including my own. I recall sorting the papers and as I reached for a page, I thought to myself, "What have I written here?" It was not my notes. The cursive writing of my grandmother had transcended time and place to be found in my own hand. A warm smile came to my face – the script style writes our bloodlines.

I will call her Grannie for that is how my mother would speak of her – Grannie Bunda. And in the process of telling some of the fragments of the fragments, she will be more than a functionary record of the archives, as I will speak with her and be with her in the writing of this story. It is a technique that I have previously used in my writing (Bunda, 2007): an intercept, a disruption – to silencing and forgetting – a tactic for giving meaning to her life.

My Grannie was born at the turn of last century, not long after the Act (1897) came into play. She was born into a social and political horrorscape for Aboriginal peoples. An 1874 Legislative Assembly report on the Aborigines of Queensland, as compiled through submissions by colonial residents, notes the number, present condition and prospects of "Aborigines" (the language of the coloniser) in each region, and advises as to the best means of improving their (Aboriginal peoples') condition. The report also identifies that "the condition" was "to make their labour useful to the settlers and profitable to themselves".

And that

> these papers have been prepared with much care by persons well acquainted with the Aborigines, and anxious for their welfare, and contain much interesting information of a race the great majority of whom, whatever may be done to improve their condition, there is too much reason to fear, are doomed to an early extinction.

The report is a clear example of how notions of welfare and concern for improving the condition of Aboriginal peoples were tied up in using our old people as cheap labour. The "profitable to themselves" part, we know, did not eventuate. Adding to this view, Social Darwinism twines itself around the articulations, strangling our mob into self-fulfilling colonial-pursued prophecies, slowly but surely taking the life out of our ancestors' lives.

In this horrorscape, my Grannie was walked from her country to incarceration at Barambah (Cherbourg). *Oh, Grannie, walking all that way. Were you frightened? Tired? Were they cruel?*

She spoke her language and when her son was born she taught him her language. She told him stories. And her stories, and her mother's stories, became his stories, told in language, told in private spaces to him, where the speaking of language in whispers could not be heard by the white authorities and punishment would be avoided. She taught him well and he inhaled the breath of her stories, absorbing them on his skin, in his heart, reaching to his young boy warrior spirit within, grounding him to his sovereign self. *Grannie, can you tell me the stories and teach me lingo?*

The regulations of the Act were thorough – new forms of scarification on the Aboriginal body. Archival documents show records of her wages, never seen, held in the Natives Savings Account. Never spent by her, sometimes in credit, sometimes in debit, always controlled by the settlement authorities. A 1933 *Report on the Books and Accounts of the Cherbourg Aboriginal Settlement* is checked by a handwritten note seen at the top of the page. It reads,

> Examples listed in the Murgon (being the closest town to Cherbourg) report disclose that the transactions in respect of the issue of stores is very unsatisfactory.

An incarceration so complete that the "settlement", through anxieties for welfare, for improving conditions, through making (slave) labour useful, was also an enterprise for economic efficiencies whereby the "natives'" wages paid for stores and more. Additionally, a "settlement maintenance levy" was implemented, whereby

> every person in employment contribute one shilling per week from their wages to the settlement to assist in providing for his wife if married or his keep when out of employment.
>
> (Blake, 2001, p. 36)

The success of this system saw the levy rise to 20% of wages deducted, but no more than 3 shillings (Blake, p. 37).

In my collection, there are letters. Letters from my father to the superintendent of Cherbourg seeking permission for his mother to visit our family in Ipswich. Letters from the superintendent to the chief protector seeking verification that this would be permissible. A letter from the chief protector to Grannie, noting the inconvenience to the superintendent. A letter from my Grannie to the superintendent asking for her ration book – the administrivia for dispossessing ourselves from ourselves. *Grannie, sorry my Gran, I swear. FUCK! I can't bear to read it and hear it in my head, let alone know that you lived it. Stealing you from your country, locking you up, not giving you a decent education, sending you out to work for wages you would never see, having to take your language underground, a black tax for your own incarceration. Who are these people?*

My grandmother passed in 1950. She died of consumption. The correspondence continued still – from the police inspector to the protector, the protector to the police inspector, the hospital to the protector, the police inspector to my mother and father, my mother and father to the police inspector and to the protector, the funeral home to the protector and the protector to the funeral home. My Grannie was 49 when she died and even in death, when her last breath had gone, she was still under the Act.

### Louise

I am 49 as I read your Grannie's story, my dear sister Tracey. Through my weeping empathetic soul I try to imagine my life ending at this age, but I have such a life of privilege that it is unfathomable to be wrenched from my family, country and language – to be enslaved and to have no freedom to speak your mind, to make life choices, to even fucking visit family. And I struggle to understand the inhumane consciousness that inflicted such vile human rights abuses. How could those bastards sleep at night? They must have had the coldest of hearts: "unloved and non-loving", ontologically empty (Nicolacopoulos & Vassilacopoulos, 2014, p. 45) to not care.

Tracey, your sublime storying interweaves multiple voices making Grannie's story so embodied. We see and feel Grannie's relations with the colonising forces and with you, her unborn granddaughter who writes with the same script, who longs to be with her, who feels her lifelong unbearable pain.

I imagine that what sustained your dear Grannie is wilfulness. Wilfulness to survive, to be a sovereign being. Yet, her enactment of sovereignty (speaking language, connecting with family) would have been judged as wilful and punished: the judgement of will as a problem of others (Ahmed, 2014). My great-great-grandmother was also wrenched from family, country and language and enslaved, a hundred years earlier.

Another perverse chapter in the nation-building project of white Australia is the convict experience. Though now convict ancestry is glorified as the "humble beginnings of a greatly successful social experiment" (Nicolacopoulos & Vassilacopoulos, 2014, p. 19), my grandfather did not tell my mother and her siblings that his grandparents were transported convicts. It was only in the 1970s that it became "fashionable" for the convict stain to see the light of day. As teenagers, my mother's father's grandparents were transported to Van Diemen's Land as convicts (forced occupiers of stolen land).

In 1842, my great-great-grandmother Nancy Ann lived with her widowed mother and three siblings in a single room in Belfast. The family had no steady income. Perhaps they had moved to Belfast from the country in search of work in the booming cotton and linen industries. Perhaps that's how Nancy's father died, crushed by the brutally unsafe machinery and work conditions, leaving his wife Mary and their four children to fend for themselves. And for Nancy, from 13, this meant selling what she had (her body) and taking what was available: sugar, bear's grease and ham (well, those were the items that she was caught stealing) (Female Convicts in Van Diemen's Land Database, 2017). In early January 1842, Nancy joined forces with a local lad named Edward and they devised a plan to steal a silver plate from a Mr Sharman Moore Esquire, Falls Road, Willowbank of Belfast. The plan was to sell the plate for food to feed her family, though Mr Moore intercepted and Nancy Ann was charged and tried for robbery and burglary at Antrim, 20 miles North of Belfast, on 13 January 1842, and given a sentence of 10 years transportation to Van Diemen's Land (Archives Office of Tasmania, 2007a). Their crime was only that of poverty, in a time when property was worth more than human lives (Swiss, 2010). (In a twisted act of justice-to-come, the only property known as Willowbank on Falls Road, Belfast, now is Willowbank Youth Club with Falls Women's Centre, painted two tones of luscious purple next door.) When Nancy Ann's mother, Mary, heard her eldest daughter's sentence, she quietly sobbed within and scrapped whatever she could to pay for a scribe to write a petition against the sentence of transportation.

CRF 1842 A1 Nancy Adams Film 46

Stamped Chief Secretary's Office Jan 26 1842

His excellency the Lord Lieutenant general; and general of Ireland

May it please His Excellency the humble petition of Mary Adams
    That the daughter of petitioner Viz, Nancy Adams was tried at the Belfast quarter Sessions of the peace on Thursday the 13th Day of January for having four Candlesticks in her possession the same being the property of Mr Moore Falls Road Belfast. She was therefore found guilty and was Sentenced to Ten years transportation.
    The unfortunate girl is fifteen years old on the 23rd June last and on her being tried an indictment for three shillings and two pence halfpenny. She got nine months imprisonment for the same. Petitioner is a poor indigent widow, who being left with four small children without any means of support. Two of which children is now incumbent on her. She is left in a deplorable state without friends to do anything for her or children.
    Petitioner Most humbly Solicits His Excellency The Lord Lieutenant in His humane goodness to take Compassion on her unfortunate daughter and please to Mitigate her Sentence from that of Transportation for ten years, to whatever imprisonment on any of Her Majesty's Penitentiarys or prisons as His Excellency may seem meet. And petitioner as in duty bound will pray.

Mary Adams

Court Belfast 14th January 1842

(Female Convicts in Van Diemen's Land Database, 2017)

The reply that was sent to Mary simply stated, "The law must take its course." And that was the last Mary ever saw or knew of Nancy Ann's fate. Feeling the heart-wrenching pain of losing a daughter, I write this to my dear great-great-great-grandmother so her soul may rest.

*Dear Mary,*

*It's your great-great-great-granddaughter here. I just want to bring you peace and let you know that Nancy Ann lived a long life with nine children and hundreds of descendants.*

After her trial, Nancy Ann spent three months incarcerated in Grangegorman Prison Dublin, the first female-only prison in the British Isles (Lawlor, 2012). Knowing her sentence of transportation to an unknown territory of Van Diemen's Land, and leaving everything that she knew behind – her

family, her home, her friends, her way of life and the measly few belong-
ings she possessed – her body was the only space on which she could record
her history and her hopes. Over time, Nancy Ann used a rusty old nail to
etch into the skin above her right elbow the initials C C S P M A M C W
M and above her left elbow R R M R S R T R J D and two hearts. She
gathered what soot she could retrieve from prison lamps and rubbed it into
the wounds to create an embodied permanent trace of those she was leaving behind. Amidst those initials, perhaps the *M*s were her mother and her
sister, both named Mary. Her father was Thomas and her brother John. Or
a more sickening thought perhaps is that they were not a sovereign body
claim, but clientele claiming female-body territory through branding (Barnard, 2016) from her "two years on the town" as noted on her convict record
at the age of 15. To Nancy Ann, life was withdrawing heart and soul deep
within, and seizing available opportunities.

In the warped threads of Nancy Ann's fate, she was transported on a convict
ship called *Hope*. I imagine hope was all Nancy Ann had to hold onto. Hope
for something better. Hope for some security and some comfort. Nancy Ann
arrived in Van Diemen's Land on 17 August 1842 and was sent to the notorious
Cascades Female Factory. Her description was scientifically recorded.

> Trade: house servant. Height: 5 feet, 2 ¾ inches. Age: 16. Complex-
> ion: fresh. Head: oval. Hair: sandy brown. Visage: oval, rather small.
> Forehead: retreating. Eyebrows: dark brown, thin. Eyes: brown. Nose:
> straight. Mouth: small. Chin: small. Remarks: C C S P M A M C and W
> M above elbow on right arm and R R M R S R T R J D and two hearts
> above elbow on left arm.
>
> (Archives Office of Tasmania, 2007b)

By 1843 Nancy was assigned to Mrs Meagher as a servant, and punished
for neglect of duty on 18 April 1843, and then again on the 8 May for being
out after hours. On 21 August, she was sentenced to 6 months' hard labour
back in the Female Factory for disorderly conduct (Female Convicts in Van
Diemen's Land Database, 2017; Archives Office of Tasmania, 2007a). The
Female Factory was a harsh place of cold, hard stone cells, 12-hour hard-
labour days in cell yards washing and pulling out knots of shipping ropes until
hands were rubbed raw, with scarce food and water and coarse uniforms that
chafed skin away and were riddled with lice, fleas and vermin (Swiss, 2010).

Female convicts were purposefully sent to Van Diemen's Land as breed-
ing fodder for the oversupply of male convicts, who outnumbered women
nine to one (Swiss, 2010). And it didn't take long for ex-convict William
Neighbour (who had served 7 years for embezzlement) (Archives Office
of Tasmania, 2007c) to submit an application to marry Nancy Ann to the
Convict Department authorities for approval. Permission to marry was

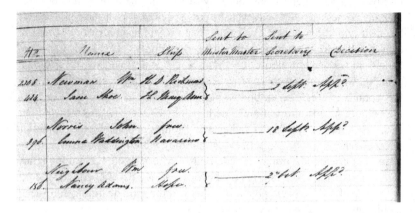

*Figure 2.2* William Neighbour and Nancy Ann Adam's Permission to Marry record.
Archives Office of Tasmania, 2007d

approved on the 27 October 1844 (Archives Office of Tasmania, 2007d). William was provided with a child-bearing mate to help populate the new colony – all part of the warped social engineering of the time.

By July 1849, they had two children, Mary Ann and William Joseph, and William senior was anxious about feeding his growing family. On his way home, he saw a sack of oats in a laneway that he thought would feed his family for at least 2 months. But as an ex-convict, William was never completely free, and so someone was always watching him. His theft saw him back in gaol for another 15 months on 1 July 1849 (Archives Office of Tasmania, 2007c). Nancy Ann was then recommended for conditional pardon on 17 July 1849 but this was not approved until the following year on 30 July 1850. By 6 January 1852, it was recognised that Nancy Ann had served her sentence and so was declared "free by servitude". Not until 28 April 1855 did Nancy Ann collect her Certificate of Freedom, which certi-fied her "free" status, by which time she had five children (Female Convicts in Van Diemen's Land Database, 2017).

Though William and Ann Neighbour (in her married life she dropped "Nancy" from her name) were now "free", they were still half citizens, sub-ject to controlled movement. They could not leave Van Diemen's Land and probably never even saw the coast, but remaining in the town they were assigned to live, Campbell Town, in central Tasmania. They were subjected to weekly headcounts after divine service on Sunday and their bank accounts were assumed by the Crown (Australian Bureau of Statistics, 2006).

Ann and William Neighbour had a total of nine children. Then, suddenly, at age 49 (the same age as your dear Grannie, Tracey), William had a heart attack on his return home from his work as a sexton at the local church in 1865. Their youngest child was only 1 year old and my great-grandfather was 3. The community gathered to support Ann and her brood and gave her the railway house, with the job of raising and dropping the boom gate when trains came through. She lived on to the grand age of 91, and her obituary in *The Daily Telegraph* (22 September 1917) referred to Mrs William Neighbour as highly respected, a native of Belfast, Ireland, and a resident of Tasmania for 75 years (Female Convicts in Van Diemen's Land Database, 2017).

In locating myself in my ancestors' storied lives, I have walked in the places they walked and seen where their remains lie, I sense their being, I sense their hardship, their pain and their extraordinary resilience. But I also know that in Nancy Ann and William's whiteness, their life chances and identities could be changed within their lifetimes. Yet the ongoing colonising discrimination of Aboriginality continues for Tracey and her family.

## Tracey responds to Louise's ancestral storying

From the penetrating gaze on Aboriginal peoples and poor vulnerable white peoples, patriarchal white sovereignty has many names. It is the magistrate's signature on the bottom of a page declaring you are to be taken away, transported away from family, friends. It is also the averted gaze of the powerful to not see, to not be involved when care is most needed by the powerless. It is the law having to take its course. I refer to Blaze Kwaymullina (2007) who says colonisation is and always was a con "shedding guilt through an intricate web of denial stories" (p. 30). If it is a con, then it is a cruel one full of coldness, thriving on disdain and intolerance for difference. Having grown up with the benefit of old people who understood the blunt force of colonisation, I was always surprised and honoured at their ability to be generous of spirit. In the full light of subjugation, these old people would have a kind word for white people's suffering. So I take up this practice and say to you, Louise, I hear your stories. I know of similar hardship of which you speak and I honour you for being troubled about your location as a white woman in the lands of Aboriginal peoples. A troubling, I acknowledge, that will often remain unspoken in black-white relationships, without a name. Our shared dialogue for knowing each other's ancestors is a good start to answering the first research questions of this country, that is, "Who's your mob and where do you come from?" And the only way to answer these questions is to tell stories. Deadly, thank you.

## Storying across cultures, times, place and space

A people without stories are a people without a history.

(Chawla, 2011, p. 16)

### *Tracey*

There is a purposefulness in telling ancestral stories through knowing our grandmothers, for there is our source. The source of our mothers, the source of ourselves, the source of our herstories. In telling my grandmother's story, I have sought to move through space, weaving words to bring me closer to her. Her story is but one sample of the many Aboriginal lives caught in the horrorscape of that time. I have also sought to make known colonisation and its sinuous trails over our countries, over our bodies. We, as Aboriginal peoples, live with the imprints that the trails leave behind, on the countries and bodies of the generations previous. But this is not a remembering complete and of itself, locked in a time past, past the point of remembering – as if finished – no more need for deep thinking. The trails are made anew, time and time again. Colonisation has not left this land and so, theoretically, Aboriginal peoples have the right to query why there is a *post* in postcolonisation. Colonisation continues and the white nations' stories of imagined freedom and liberation for Aboriginal peoples through being made civilised are told to sooth the pillow of a denying (white) race. Think of the Emergency Response in the Northern Territory (HREOC, 2007), which sought to "stabilize" Aboriginal communities and "address" family violence and child abuse. In this, we as Aboriginal peoples see yet again the sinuousness of colonising effect to administrivia – a new Aborigines Protection Act; new ways to initiate new forms of control through the introduction of the BasicsCard; new forms of dispossession from land ownership under Aboriginal community control for promised but forever-eventuating housing reform; new forms of welfarism that did away with the Community Development Employment Program for the harshly enforced Work for the Dole Programs; and new forms of "caring" for the condition of the "Aborigine" through heavy-handed alcohol restriction and compulsory health checks on children. And again, the trails are deeply imprinted with passive violence on Aboriginal bodies and minds. The basic tenets of the story of colonisation in Australia do not change across time, place and space. The story generates its own momentums through cycles and renders its presence from behind a mask, to distort the senses, disavowing Aboriginal truths. It is a story with devastating consequences, however, for Aboriginal peoples. Why does this story not change? Is it because Aboriginal truth speaking is a humanity that displaces the face mask of colonisation, revealing white nation building as an enterprise traced with untruths and violence? Which our grandmothers lived with. Which we all (Aboriginal and white) live with. Transforming this story will require constant courage and conviction – a warriorship of the soul. Perhaps, in the remembering of our old people, in knowing our ancestral stories, more is evoked than the telling of stories.

## *Louise*

Embodying ancestral stories has sprouted a deeper sense of where I come from in the troubling of uncertainty (of self and place) as a white occupier on stolen land. I have known my genealogy for 30 years, but the proposition of locating self in ancestral storying has provoked further connection with a great-great-grandmother. I have dug beyond facts to sense her lived experiences, to be there with Nancy Ann. Sensing every cut for every line of each inked initial ingrained into her skin. I have held the puncturing of needle into flesh through stitching the initials into fine cloth. Pulling at the weft and warp threads with a felting needle to embody and hold the ongoing abuse – the wear and tear of a harsh life. Submerging in tea – to reflect the aged stain of a convict record.

I have held the heart-wrenching pain of Mary Adams desperate plea to keep her daughter with her in Belfast. By disrupting time as continuous (chronological), from a quantum physics position I feel the entanglements of my life, my body with Mary's and Nancy Ann's. In quantum dis/continuity there is no overarching sense of temporality, of continuity, in place. Each scene diffracts various temporalities within and across the field of spacetimemattering. "Scenes never rest, but are reconfigured within, dispersed across and threaded through one another" (Barad, 2010, p. 240).

I walked the paths that Nancy Ann treaded in Hobart when she arrived in Van Diemen's Land – the grounds of the Female Factory, the neighbouring streets and lanes. I sensed Nancy Ann's focus on the task at hand (be it washing, cleaning, collecting groceries), and her tenacious resilience. Only the surrounding walls of the Female Factory remain, though the embedded pain in stone walls lingers and a dark, heavy cloud of deep misery weighs heavily over the site. Scenes that never rest.

By threading past, present and future through one another, an integrative depth of sense of self and place is woven. "The 'past' and the 'future' are iteratively reworked and enfolded through the iterative practices of spacetimemattering" (Barad, 2010, pp. 260–261). Locating self in ancestral storying is an iterative reworking and enfolding of past, present and future, that is, spacetimemattering.

But what lingers most is the soullessness of ontological emptiness – the hardened disconnect of the colonial subject – of feeling unloved and unable

*Figure 2.3* Stitched armband of initials and hearts on Nancy Ann's left arm.
Photograph taken by Tracey.

to love. Feminism, sisterhood and stories have given me some sense of belonging, some sense of joy, values and passion that are coldly absent from the colonial subject. And I have sought, throughout my adult life, to nurture embodied and spiritual connections to the land and waters upon which I live, work, walk and visit. I have sought out the wisdom of this ancient land, by seeking out the ancient stories that tell of how this place came to be, how each creature came to be and their relationships with each other. I have done this by listening to Elders about how to feel every breath of every living thing, and by completing every Aboriginal studies unit that was available in my undergraduate degree. I have soaked up the great wisdom and pleasure of walking country with dear Aboriginal friends. In essence, to locate some sense of belonging I have sought out (and continue to seek out) the ancient wisdom of the land, a recommended remedy for displaced people to nurture belonging (Blackie, 2016).

Further holding of the past in the present through storying is reflected in the metonymic *logos* epitome of "cinders there are" proposed by Derrida (1991) for "which holds all beings and entities in the presence" (p. 1)

– though they are only momentarily in the present, as a cinder "immediately incinerates in front of your eyes" (p. 35), its delicate tenderness diminishing to dust. In storying, the people, places and time are alive – full embodied sensation and perception. Then the dust settles and lingers. Places occur so they will be understood. "Cinders there are: Place there is" (p. 37). The cinder is suggestive of what lurks beneath – "Incubation of the fire lurking beneath the dust" (p. 59). The energy of the storytelling (the fire) retreats, leaving the cinders, the diminishing dust, as the intensity of the story's presence dissipates but never completely vanishes: cinders remain. Derrida, like Barad, read the world as entangled matter:

> Our entire world is the cinder of innumerable living beings; and what is living is so little in relation to the whole, it must be that, once already, everything was transformed into life and it will continue to be so.
>
> (p. 69)

Through storying, we come to live, breath and feel deep penetrating understandings of identity and place.

## Together/two-gather

Storying our ancestral stories has been a process that has spanned months, years. A process of gathering data from family members telling us stories, from searching in archives and reading historical fiction and nonfiction from times and places of our ancestors. Then mulling over these pieces of data across days, weeks, months. The mulling seeds questions and makes links between pieces of data. We verbally story the data with others. And in time, when the energy of the stories demands, we start to compose words on pages. At first loosely mapped, and then revisited again and again, slowly fleshing out the heart and soul of the story.

Locating self in ancestral storying feeds into what is referred to as a research positionality or standpoint, so that the reader knows what position you bring, what standpoint you take to the phenomena of inquiry. Yet it yields so much more. As Pinkola Estes (1992) explains, so many of us are lost, hungering for numinous experience, exacerbated because we have lost our ancestors, not knowing names and origins beyond grandparents, and not knowing family stories, values and practices. She declares that "spiritually, this situation causes sorrow . . . and hunger" (p. 208). With the strength of entanglement with ancestors and a myriad of other beings, we declare the standpoints we bring to storying. We stand for human rights, not a liberal individualist view of rights but a collectivist view for children, for women, for Indigenous peoples, for refugees. Our reflections on ancestral storying here have led us to think through what can be the principles for storying which we speak to in the following chapter.

## References

*Aboriginal Protection and Restriction of the Sale of Opium Act 1897* (Qld). Retrieved from www.foundingdocs.gov.au/resources/transcripts/qld5_doc_1897.pdf

Ahmed, S. (2005). The politics of bad feeling. *Australian Critical Race and Whiteness Studies Association Journal, 1*, 72–85.

Ahmed, S. (2014). *Willful subjects*. London: Duke University Press.

Archives Office of Tasmania. (2007a). *Digitised record item: CON40–1–2*. Retrieved from http://search.archives.tas.gov.au/ImageViewer/image_viewer.htm?CON40-1-2,266,24,F,60

Archives Office of Tasmania (2007b). *Digitised record item: CON19-1-3*. Retrieved from http://search.archives.tas.gov.au/ImageViewer/image_viewer.htm?CON19-1-3,230,135,F,52

Archives Office of Tasmania (2007c). *Digitised record item: CON31-1-33*. Retrieved from http://search.archives.tas.gov.au/ImageViewer/image_viewer.htm?CON31-1-33,152,57,F,60

Archives Office of Tasmania (2007d). *Digitised record item: CON52-1-2p069*. Retrieved from https://stors.tas.gov.au/CON52-1-2p069

Australian Bureau of Statistics. (2006). *Census history in Tasmania*. Retrieved from www.abs.gov.au/ausstats/abs@.nsf/7d12b0f6763c78caca257061001cc588/7ece0 45bc4080344ca256c320024164d!OpenDocument

Australian Institute of Aboriginal and Torres Strait Islander Studies. (2017). *Research*. Retrieved from http://aiatsis.gov.au/sites/default/files/docs/family_ history_kit/Sources-birth-death-marriage-records.pdf

Barad, K. (2010). Quantum entanglements and hauntological relations of inheritance: Dis/continuities, spacetime enfoldings, and justice-to-come. *Derrida Today, 3*(2), 240–268.

Barnard, S. (2016). *Convict tattoos: Marked men and women of Australia*. Melbourne, Australia: Text Publishing.

Beaglehole, J. C. (Ed.). (1955). *The journals of Captain James Cook on his voyages of discovery*, Vol. 1, the voyage of the Endeavour, 1768–1771. Surrey, UK: Hakluyt Society.

Blackie, S. (2016). *If women rose rooted: The journey to authenticity and belonging*. London: September Publishing.

Blake, T. (2001). *A dumping ground: A history of the Cherbourg settlement*. St Lucia: University of Queensland Press.

Bunda, T. (2007). The sovereign Aboriginal woman. In A. Moreton-Robinson (Ed.), *Sovereign subjects: Indigenous sovereignty matters*. Crows Nest, NSW: Allen & Unwin.

Bunda, T. (2014). *The relationship between Indigenous peoples and the university: Solid or what!* (Doctoral thesis). University of South Australia, Australia.

Champney, J., & Pickering, J. (1997). *One hundred and forty years of our brook family in Australia 1856–1996.* Australia: Author.

Chawla, D. (2011). Between stories and theories embodiments, disembodiments, and other struggles. In D. Chawla & A. Rodriguez (Eds.), *Liminal traces: Storying, performing, and embodying postcoloniality* (Vol. 72, pp. 13–24). Rotterdam, The Netherlands: Sense Publishers.

Colebrook, C. (2008). Narrative happiness and the meaning of life. *New Formations, 63,* 85–102.

Derrida, J. (1991). *Cinders* (N. Lukacher, Trans.). Lincoln: University of Nebraska Press.

Estes, C. P. (1992). *Women who run with the wolves: Contacting the power of the wild woman.* London: Rider.

Haraway, D. (1991). *Simians, cyborgs, and women.* New York: Routledge.

hooks, b. (1995). Writing autobiography. In M. Blair, J. Holland, & S. Sheldon (Eds.), *Identity and diversity: Gender and the experience of education* (pp. 3–7). Clevedon, UK: Multilingual Matters.

Human Rights and Equal Opportunity Commission. (2007). *Social justice report chapter 3: The Northern Territory emergency response intervention* (Report No. 1/2008). Retrieved from www.humanrights.gov.au/publications/social-justice-report-2007-chapter-3-northern-territory-emergency-response-intervention

Keirs, R. G. (1997). *A promised land: A family history of early Queensland settlers* (2nd ed.). Lidcombe, NSW: Author.

Kristeva, J. (1981). Women's time (A. Jardine & H. Blake, Trans.). *Signs, 7*(1), 13–35.

Kwaymullina, B. (2007). Introduction: Listening through the heart. In S. Morgan, M. Tjalaminu, & B. Kwaymullina (Eds.), *Speaking from the heart stories of life, family and country.* Fremantle, Western Australia: Fremantle Arts Press Centre.

Langton, M. (1993). *"Well, I heard it on the radio and I saw it on the television": An essay for the Australian film commission on the politics and aesthetics of filmmaking by and about Aboriginal people and things.* North Sydney, NSW: Australian Film Commission.

Lawlor, R. (2012). *Crime in nineteenth-century Ireland: Grangegorman female penitentiary and Richmond male penitentiary, with reference to juveniles and women, 1836–60* (Doctoral thesis). National University of Ireland Maynooth, Ireland.

Logan City Council. (2017). *Slacks Creek.* Retrieved from www.logan.qld.gov.au/about- logan/suburbs/slacks-creek

Native Names. (1898, December 17). *Evening news (Sydney, NSW: 1869–1931),* p. 8 (EVENING NEWS CHRISTMAS NUMBER). Retrieved from http://nla.gov.au/nla.news-article114041354

Nicolacopoulos, T., & Vassilacopoulos, G. (2014). *Indigenous sovereignty and the being of the occupier: Manifesto for a white Australian philosophy of origins.* Melbourne: Re.Press.

Nye, A., Barker, L., & Charteris, J. (2016). Matrilineal narratives: Learning from voices and objects. *Hecate: An Interdisciplinary Journal of Women's Liberation, 41*(1/2), 180–190.

Queensland Legislative Assembly. (1874). *Aborigines of Queensland: Report of the commissioners.* Retrieved from http://nla.gov.au/nla.obj-53959500

Radstone, S. (2010). Nostalgia: Home-comings and departures. *Memory Studies,3*(3), 187–191.

Renwick, W. (Ed.). (1991). *Sovereignty and indigenous rights: The treaty of Waitangi in international contexts.* Wellington: Victoria University Press.

Reynolds, H. (1999). *Why weren't we told? A personal search for the truth about our history.* Ringwood, VIC: Viking Press.

Roberts, J. (1981). *Massacres to mining: The colonisation of Australia.* Blackburn, VIC: Dove Communications.

Swiss, D. (2010). *Tin ticket: The heroic journey of Australia's convict women.* New York: Berkley Publishing Group.

Trask, H.-K. (1993). *From a native daughter: Colonialism and sovereignty in Hawai'i.* Honolulu: University of Hawaii Press.

Van Diemen's Land Database. (2017). *Nancy Adams entry 811.* Retrieved from http://itsfilemaker2.its.utas.edu.au/fmi/webd#Female_Convicts_in_VDL_database

# 3　Principles of storying

So far you have come to know that we connect through story. We understand self, country/place and others through story. More and more academics are using the term *storying* in titles to describe their work. There are thousands of entries in online searches. More and more research students across the globe are being drawn to storying. The practice of storying is emergent and responsive, so we purposefully refuse to offer a prescriptive formula for storying. Yet we are well aware that when starting out as a researcher, guidance and direction are sought. Consequently, from mulling over what is central to storying for more than a year, we have located five *principles of storying*. They are (1) storying nourishes thought, body and soul; (2) storying claims voice in the silenced margins; (3) storying is embodied relational meaning making; (4) storying intersects the past and present as living oral archives; and (5) storying enacts collective ownership and authorship. This is not a definitive list. We propose these principles as prevalent to our storying work at the time of writing this book. In the emergent practice of storying, we acknowledge that these principles will continue to morph slowly through intersections with others. But what remains constant and integral to all of these principles is place or country. Stories and storying are located. Country and place provide the fertile soil for the stories to seed. Country and place holds the stories. But first, Tracey stories.

## Tracey

On a visit to my daughter's families in the desert we stopped at the art co-op and bought Kathleen Wallace's book, *Listen Deeply, Let These Stories In*. A precious book, full of Kathleen's artwork, stories, language and photographs. I know my daughter holds a deep admiration for Kathleen, who is an artist and educator, just as my daughter is. In the foreword of her book, Kathleen eloquently speaks about many of the notions of what we are calling *the principles of storying*. In seeing and hearing her words there

DOI: 10.4324/9781315109190-3

is nourishment for the body and soul, and embodied meaning making. The past combines with the present to be a living archive and there is collective authorship. Kathleen writes,

> The stories I'm sharing with you in this book . . . don't belong to me alone. They were told to me by my grandparents . . . and by some of my aunts and uncles – and other elders too, such as my husband . . . and his father . . . There were many of our old people living here in the old days and these stories come from all of them, from their ancestors and before that from the altyerrenge, the time when the first beings created Arrernte people and our world. They're stories from my grandparents' country, our homelands . . . from all those places and other places around here. The stories I'll tell you are about some of these places, the ancestor days, the spirits of those places and something of my life as I grew up . . . I listened to a lot of the stories and I remembered many of them – I let those stories come into me. I thought really hard about them. They taught me many things. They stayed with me when I was living out bush as a young person, they kept me going, surviving, and knowing my own family and culture. The stories taught me about myself too. When we lost our bush life, they held me together through all the changes.
>
> (pp. ix–xi)

Our work is emplaced in Australia and notions of country, known and understood in Aboriginal senses, with deep connections of body to land being situated beside white senses of the notion of place. The density of this relationship is in a state of constant becoming; however, with generosity of spirit, Kathleen's words invite the reader to engage, to be present, to learn of self, to learn in stories from the stories of First Peoples – an invitational and methodology for sharing.

### Principle: storying nourishes thought, body and soul

> What ought to be interesting . . . is the unfolding of a lived life rather than the confirmation such a chronicle provides for some theory . . . Let the story itself be our discovery.
>
> (Coles, 1989, p. 22)

We experience stories as theories and, like Devika Chawla (2011), locate our "theoretical roots in a storied world" (p. 13). We know we are not alone (e.g., see Chawla, 2011; Quintero & Rummel, 2015). We are drawn into stories. We imagine that we are there, and through that vicarious encounter are affected and wonder. The stories that we encounter stay with us and we muse over them, new insights unfurling over time. We make meaning through story. The metaphors and motifs of stories offer layers of symbolism that we unwrap over time.

Theory is often argued for and presented in masculine ways in academia. Its presence is demanded and forced: "You've got to have theory." "It has no weight if there's no theory." We recognise that for many, theory is unkind and exclusionary. For example, Devika Chawla (2011), a South Asian Indian woman living in middle America, wrote of her "resistance/s to theory" and her "leanings toward 'storying'" and the ongoing struggle to reside in the liminal space between stories and theories (p. 6). As she later explains,

> I was not born into theory. I don't believe that theory was embedded into the world in which I grew up. If it was then I remained unaware of it. At the same time, I was also not raised in a home environment where the word "theory" was ever a part of spoken vocabulary.
>
> (Chawla, 2011, p. 13)

Chawla declares her resistance to theory as rooted in her family and educational heritage. Theory is language of the intellectual elite, and our movement to storying is to enable accessibility to theory – to give uplift to stories as the tools of research. Our claim is that storying has long read the world, and in its existence there is theory. Cultures across times have ontological stories (e.g., Aboriginal Dreaming stories, Greek myths, Hindu myths) that are passed from generation to generation and communicate theories of how to live, how to be human. They are timeless stories that are layered with meaning through symbolism and metaphor. They are theories used to explain phenomena. There is a cautionary note here in the use of the concept of "Dreaming", which is often mobilised in simplistic and incorrect ways within dominant ways of knowing Aboriginal peoples, traditions and practices. These deny Aboriginal meanings and understandings through a discourse that reduces the phenomenon of Aboriginal spirituality being to the "mythical and not real" – that is, the Aboriginal Dreaming of a past and imagined spiritual life that supposedly no longer has relevance in "modern" times and spaces. We do not agree with this viewpoint. Stories matter and endure.

Irene Watson, Tanganekald and Meintangk woman of the Coorong, lawyer and academic, invokes the ancient law story of the greedy frog who drank up all the water in her essay "Aboriginal Laws and the Sovereignty of *Terra Nullius*" (2002). The spirits who lived with the greedy frog suffered without the water and made the decision to make the frog laugh to release the water back into the land. Watson, in her writing, demonstrates the greed and thoughtlessness of *krinkri* (white) law. Despite the 1992 legal decision of Mabo that placed the colonising story of *terra nullius* into fiction, multiple manifestations of the legal doctrine of *terra nullius* continue. *Krinkri* law remains unsatisfied – the frog keeps on drinking and the First People of spirit, Aboriginal peoples, remain thirsty for rights. The primary meaning mapped into the law story of the frog speaks to the life value of sharing, that greed as a dominating ethos denies and subjugates and to be lawful is to be embodied in country. The law connects to people, and people to land. Stories are a central means of defining law and remembering traditions among Aboriginal people. The message in this story is a reminder that in Aboriginal law there is thoughtfulness for the body and soul which in turn is inextricably connected to land. In neglect, Aboriginal and white positions in relations of power in contestations over who has sovereignty in land/country are left unbalanced through the construction and maintenance of difference and separation. Jo-ann Archibald of the Stol:lo nation, in her seminal work *Indigenous Storywork*, reminds us that stories have the power to make our hearts, minds and bodies work together (2008, p. 12). Remembering the story of the greedy frog has significance beyond dreaming/Dreaming the mythical, and as Watson demonstrates, the story has deep and theoretical meaning.

Political philosopher Hannah Arendt's work (1906–1975) has contributed significantly to the foregrounding of story in academia. Hannah was widely known for her love of telling stories:

> A charming disregard for mere facts (se non e evero, e bene travoto [even if it is not true, it is well conceived]) and unfailing regard for the life of the story . . . her stories and her sayings were the threads with which she wove her conversations and her works.
>
> (Young-Bruehl, 1977, p. 183)

From the dark times she lived in (she experienced the holocaust as a Germanic Jew), she gathered threads (thought fragments) to create stories that were "dynamic, and illuminating" (p. 183), offering astute observations (*aphoras*). This is what we mean by storying as theory. Storying has the capacity to activate a plurality of possible meanings that multiplies significance, yet resists closure. This is the beauty of storying. There is no one way to understand the theory stories offer – the integrative nourishment offered to mind, body and soul.

In research through, with and as storying, control over the story's meaning is relinquished, with listeners/viewers/readers welcomed to bring their own interpretations, understandings and sensibilities to bear on the story told (Barone, 1995). In storying we are engaging in analytical thinking, we are selecting data, we are interpreting, we are evoking theory and crafting stories to make meaning. We argue that stories tell what "no amount of theorizing or recitation of statistics" could reveal – they offer insight that generates empathy and builds social bonds (Duncan, 1998, p. 107). Compelling stories connect personal experience to broader societal discourses (Berger & Quinney, 2005). Stories become embodied, challenge our thinking and nurture our spirits.

## Tracey

I have had the fortune of watching Louise tell the following story, and in the performance I have seen the audience captured. Louise uses her body to shape the winds of dislocation and throws herself literally to land with a thud on the floor. Stories are not often told in academic settings. In this instance – a national conference – there is rupturing of the rigidity and formality of these spaces, yet there is a genuine appreciation by the audience of being caught up in the words, to hear, feel, guess at where this story is going and why.

## Louise stories: "The Man Who Had No Story"

This is an Irish story from the Irish tendril of my ancestry. It was not passed down, but located in *The Penguin Book of Irish Folktales* (Glassie, 1993) that I purchased in a village on the east coast of Ireland more than 20 years ago. It's the last story in the book. I can't recall if I read every story in the book, but I more suspect that I was drawn in by the title for its absurdist proposition – "The Man Who Had No Story". An imagined impossibility or an absurdist piece on a droll life. I relished every word when I read it, and thus chose to add it to my storytelling repertoire for adult storytelling gatherings and for opening workshops on storytelling with children. The embedded provocative messages resonated, offering ontological and epistemological theories. I have probably performed this story a hundred times now. Though I drew from Glassie's versions, my hands are all over the story now, shaped with my worldview and words. Here goes:

*There once was a man named Brian. He lived in Ireland when times were really tough. The English had taken over everything. Brian wove baskets for a living, but it had become harder and harder to source wicker or rods to weave with, because as I said, the English had taken over everything. Now Brian knew of a faery glen where he was sure he would find plenty of wicker and rods. You know the faeries I mean. The wicked Irish faeries. But Brian daren't go in there for fear of what the faeries might do to him. And so Brian searched high and low for wicker and rods until it came to the time when there was no other choice but to go into the faery glen. He declared to his wife his intentions and she kindly packed him some lunch (wives did such things back then), which he bundled up with some rope and a hook and then he set off into the faery glen. Now he didn't get far into the glen before a fog set in, and he thought he would stop and eat his lunch in the hope that the fog would lift by the time he finished. However, by the time he finished, he couldn't even see his own hand in front of his face. Then suddenly, a great wind came and blew him this way and that and landed him with a great thud on the ground.*

*Brian looked around to see if he could see anything and in the distance, he saw a light. Now he knew that where there was light there must be people, so he walked slowly towards it. As he got closer he saw a house, and when he got to the entrance he saw an old man and an old woman sitting by a fire. She beckoned for him to come and sit with them. Once he was seated she said to him, "Now have you got a story tell us then, love?" Startled by the request Brian promptly replied, "Nay. I've never told a story in m' life."*

*"Well, take this bucket down to the well and fill it for us, dear."*

*"Aye," Brian nodded, anything but tell a story. And so, he took the bucket down to the well and filled it, and just as he was steadying it on the side of the well, a great wind came and blew him this way and that and he landed with a great thud.*

*Brian looked around to locate himself. And he saw a light. Now he knew that where there is light there must be people. So he walked towards the light. And as he got closer he saw a longhouse, and when he got to the doorway he saw people sitting all around the edges of the long room. A young lady with curly black hair gestured to him to come and sit beside her, which he did rather coyly; he was a married man after all. The young lady explained to Brian that this was a wake for a very important man of the village. The big man of the gathering came over to say that he was going into town to get a fiddler, as it was going to be a long night. The young lady said, "O, there is no need. We have Brian here tonight."*

*"Nay!" Brian declared. "I have never played the fiddle in my life." But before he knew it, they thrust a fiddle into his hands. And he played and he played the most delightful tunes, and everyone danced and danced. And they all declared Brian the greatest fiddler in the whole of Ireland. Then the big man said the dancing must stop because it was time to get the priest for the funeral service. The young lady said, "O, there is no need we have Brian here tonight. He tells the finest funeral service."*

*"Nay!" said Brian. "I've never been to seminary school or anything." But before he knew it, they had placed a priest's holy vestment across his shoulders and he began to speak the most beautiful words. Everyone had tears streaming down their cheeks. And they all applauded his sermon as the finest they had ever heard.*

*Then it was time to carry the coffin to the cemetery. And as the pallbear-*
*ers gathered it so happened that one pallbearer was much taller than the*
*others. The young lady with the curly black hair declared that there was*
*naught to worry about as Brian was here and he is the finest surgeon in the*
*whole of Ireland.*

*"Nay!" said Brian. "I've never been to medical school or anything." But*
*before he knew it, they placed a scalpel in his hand and laid the tall man*
*down. Brian cut a section from both the tall man's calves and restitched*
*them together with stitches so fine that you would never know there had*
*been an incision. The whole funeral procession declared Brian was the fin-*
*est surgeon in the whole of Ireland. And the pallbearers regathered – now*
*all of equal height – and carried the coffin to the cemetery. Brian was last*
*in the funeral procession. They had to climb over a stone wall to enter the*
*cemetery and when Brian was on top of the wall, a great wind came and*
*blew him this way and that and then he landed with a thud.*

*He looked around to locate himself, and there was the well, with the*
*bucket he had filled still perched on the rim. He collected it and took into*
*the old woman and man. And the old woman said, "Well, have you got a*
*story to tell then, love?"*

*"Aye, aye," said Brian and he told them the story of where he had been*
*and what had happened. The old woman and the old man thought it was the*
*greatest story they had ever heard. They gave him some food and he rested.*
*When he awoke he was in the glen and beside him was his empty lunch*
*container and his rope, wound around a great bundle of rods and wicker.*
*He picked them up and set off home. When he got home he told his wife the*
*story. She too thought it was the greatest story she had ever heard. And so,*
*when he went to the markets to sell his newly made baskets, Brian told many*
*market-goers the story, and pretty soon Brian became known as the greatest*
*storyteller in the whole of Ireland.*

The theory this story speaks to me has evolved over time, and varies according to my presence of mind when being with the story. The most resonant
theory is that of risk, of trying the new against your beliefs that you do not
know or cannot do. What psychologist Susan Jeffers' *Feel the Fear and
Do It Anyway* (1987) took a whole book to discuss and unpack, "The Man
Who Had No Story" offers in a 10-minute story. Following on from the
theory of risk is the theory of entering dark, unknown spaces on a quest – a
common motif in narratology and folklore, and a good storytelling technique to build suspense, but also symbolic of working through uncertainty
and mystery. There is the tease and taunt of treading the fine line between
pleasing or displeasing the faeries, and in turn, being rewarded or cursed.
The presence of the faeries cranks up the intensity of life's performance,

inviting an increased consciousness of actions to consider others. And in being comfortable in the unknown, I see the theory of being open to trying roles beyond our scope – even what might seem the impossible (e.g., cutting a section of a man's legs off and having him immediately walking again). The accompanying theory of encouraging nudges supports those leaps of faith. These theories are punctuated with a theory of wind-spurred displacement, and closes with a theory of hope for unassuming greatness.

Okay, the sceptic reader might be thinking, these are just the morals or metaphors of the story. Morals and metaphors explain something just as theories do, but through implicit illustrative experiences. The intent of theory is to explain. The intent of story is to illustrate through symbolism and invite the listener/reader to ponder, to draw out the theories that are relevant to them. I avoid the use of the word *moral* as it suggests a lesson in a didactic and moralistic sense. And I avoid stories of such nature, such as biblical tales. Rather, I am drawn to stories with more suggestive, obscure symbolism in which the listener/reader has agency. Stories with subtle symbolism can be used to generate theory from "ordinary experiences" (The Res-Sisters, 2017), as well as the extraordinary.

In sum, we relish storying for the integrative nourishment offered for our minds, bodies and souls. We argue that it has a place in all sectors of society. Storying is not less-than in academia, but actually equal-to. In fact, for the connoisseur of theories beyond the well-worn, storying research is more-than. There is theory, there is rigour, there is trustworthiness, there is validity, but there is also pleasure. Storying is enjoyable to read, view and listen, and storying unashamedly honours emotions and spirit (expressions often taboo in academic circles). Through storying, we then can develop deeper, more complex understanding of phenomena.

### Principle: storying claims voice in the silenced margins

We see storying as practice that can claim voice in the silenced margins and counter metanarratives. That is, it offers a legitimate alternative to widely held narratives such as " 'monovocal' stories about the low educational achievement and attainment of students of color are told" (Solórzano & Yosso, 2002, p. 27). In his critique of modernism, Lyotard (1984) explained how metanarratives shape knowledge, and grow in strength having oppressive, exclusionary and totalising effects as they work to explain a concept rather than just tell the story of an event. We see potential in stories, particularly stories from the margins, as pushing back against oppressive and exclusionary metanarratives, be they about research, academia or society at large. The work of counter stories does this.

Chicana feminist theorist Gloria Anzaldúa (1990) adds her voice to this argument. She writes,

> Social issues such as race, class, and sexual difference are intertwined with the narrative and poetic elements of a text, elements in which theory is embedded. In our mestizaje [mixed ancestries] theories we create new categories for those of us left out or pushed out of existing ones.
>
> (p. xxvi)

And more pointedly, Solórzano and Yosso (2002) note that counter stories are stories of people on the margins. We use critical theories to frame storying research. Given the racialised nature of Australia, critical race theory (CRT) gives us voice to interrogate the intersectionalities of race and power, to make known Aboriginal standpoints for exposing the everyday racisms and privileges of whiteness. Ladson-Billings (1998) nominates that "this is important as social reality is constructed by the formulation and exchange of stories with the 'voices' of raced/marginalised groups being able to name lived realities" (p. 13). Counter stories are not created and voiced only in response to metanarratives or majoritarian stories. By doing such, those grand narratives still dominate the discourse (Ikemoto, 1997; Solórzano & Yosso, 2002). We, like Solórzano and Yosso, look to a broader appeal of counter stories in which the histories and lived experiences of people on the margins are shared to "strengthen traditions of social, political, and cultural survival and resistance" (p. 32). Drawing from Delgado (1989) and Lawson (1995), Solórzano and Yosso (2001) also identify that counter stories can perform "at least four theoretical, methodological, and pedagogical functions", in broad brushstrokes, they build community; challenge perceived wisdom; open windows to the realities at the margins and show possibilities for those at the margin; and they teach others to construct another world that is richer than either the story or the reality alone (p. 475).

There are many counter stories that speak back to metanarratives of Aboriginal peoples. The stories are an intended disruption to dominant practices for knowing Aboriginal peoples. They demonstrate how struggles inform identities and agencies necessary to counter those representations that seek to limit. Through these stories, there is a critical unravelling of what it means to identify as Aboriginal in Australia. These stories are an important centring of Aboriginal critical voices that speak to lived experiences, contributing to understandings of power in, and over, Aboriginal lives. The holding of stories in heads and hearts and the telling of these stories about power have been fundamental to Aboriginal cultural and political survival. These stories, shared between and across generations, inform Aboriginal knowing and being. White people are too often the only authorities of Aboriginal lives and histories. So powerful is the dominant colonial storying of Aboriginal peoples that the possibility of Aboriginal people having their own stories – and moreover, stories that are imbued with theoretical positions – is rendered impossible, flung to a margin to be out of sight and out of the colonisers' minds or, when heard, disavowed. Aboriginal people are not all assimilated and have not all forgotten. In this book, Aboriginal stories are intentionally privileged.

## Tracey stories: "Taken"

*In 1929 a black mother, desperate, powerless and tormented, came to the local white legal authorities. She carried with her the unfathomable guilt and shame of a crime committed by her spouse. She held to the belief that treading a path to the door of the* gunjis *would hold to the real possibility that her family would be protected from the violence within. An impossible possibility to believe that a white system's love of its own superior sense of reasoning would reach across and seamlessly meld with her aching need. The pain in her heart disavowed risk. A desperate black mother enacting an aching need in desperate times, desperately wanting to rewrite the colonial script that hung ominously in her life, sometimes as backdrop, sometimes threatening to smother all of her life.*

*In this colonial script, the words* Aboriginal *and* mother *spoken in the same breath were treated with scepticism. Black mothers were neglectful in mothering. This was an often-cited verse of white logic, shaped in a continuing colonising context that could not – and would not – meld with the illogical coupling of "the black" and "the mother". The risk, initially disavowed, that was held silently within the black mother, rose quickly, visibly, to its full height. Torment added to torment. What answers could the white system of policing and justice provide for her pain? How to alleviate the pain? With more pain? An ordinance was drawn decreeing that the three eldest children needed to be "taken".*

*A small ramshackle house of rusting corrugated tin, slapped-together old timber boards for walls and a dirt floor could be found down the bush track. It is away from the town that bustles with its own importance and only becomes known, is seen, when the lives inside the shack have percussion with the important things of that town where white people live. The bush track, lined with white gums and scrubby bush that have taken shape from too many battles with the wind, travels parallel to the sea. Pale-blue skies, slow-moving puffed-up clouds and a taste of salt in the air paints a picture complete.*

*The shack ordinarily holds a messy tangle of children, lean of body and light of feet. Some of that messy tangle is outside, playing imaginary games that will keep them occupied for hours and days and weeks. Inside, on the iron-framed bed strangled tight with a grey blanket, GOVERNMENT stamped in red, sit the three.*

*The youngest is aware that this not another ordinary day. If it were, she would be outside with the other siblings. Her oldest brother fixes his eyes to look at nothing but everything in particular. There is not much to look at. Her older sister is almost silently crying. Tears well up and roll down, leaving track marks on her cheeks. She watches how the tracks are made, following the shape of her sister's face, down her cheeks to the jawline, to be soaked up in her skin or to be wiped away by a torn square of once white-coloured rag that doubles for a handkerchief. The youngest looks for answers. What makes her older sister cry? What makes her older brother's face so resolute?*

*Her mother, tall and white haired, holds her pannikin of tea with both hands, and from her position at the table looks out the only window to the track outside in the bush. Even with the little light that seeps through the glass pane of the window, she can tell that her mother's face is off-colour. Today it holds an ashen grey in the thin folds of deep-brown worry. Thinking the answer is outside, the youngest stretches her neck and looks in that direction too. There is nothing to see but the same old bush, so she gives up straining and instead concentrates on her feet as she makes them methodically swing up and back from the edge of the bed. She won't fall; she has her sister's hand to keep her steady.*

*Her concentration is broken by the movement of her mother's chair. Her mother shifts her body and simultaneously motions her legs out from the table. As she rises, the youngest knows that this is a response to the car engine she hears, they all hear, making its way down the track. Stretching her neck again she sees a black car with silver trim bumping along, and her younger brothers and sister racing to meet it. Her sister's hand that holds her own grows tighter and she feels her fingers crushing. Her sister's other hand reaches for their eldest brother, but he has already moved off the bed and towards their mother. Together, the four make their way out of the house, outside into the brightness, and to the sound of tyres padding the dirt as the car comes to come a stop.*

*A white man opens the car door, steps out and makes his way to her mother with a piece of paper in hand. His clothes and manner mark him as important. The importance of the white town has come to her family. With her elder brother and sister, she climbs into the back seat of the car. Her sister's crying is now inconsolable sobs. The white man driving navigates the car back onto the track and they leave the bush and the sea, the younger brothers, sister and mother behind. She has been taken. The three have been taken away.*

*Standing at the end of that dirt track, she watches as the three are being taken from her life. Taken to be given an education, taken to be civilised, taken "for their own good". A white system, objective in its reasoning, brought justice for her, for her first three. How? Where is the logic? A logic that is limited to itself, a logic that lacks. A logic without the possibility to embrace the desperate desire of the black mother to care for her children.*

*On the colonial orders of providing the three with "protection" and "education" they were taken by white authorities south to Brisbane, and then west to the Salvation Army–managed Aboriginal mission of Purga, located outside of Ipswich. On arrival, the three who had endured a strange and terrorising kidnapping were separated again. The oldest boy was placed in the boys' dormitory, whilst the two girls were placed in another dormitory. The youngest of the three had arrived in Purga. It was her birthday. She was 7.*

This is the story of my mother. It was she who was taken with her brother and sister. I have reproduced the archival documentation – the orders to take my mum, aunt and uncle, as follows:

Archival Transcript
30/4542 Industrial School
Brisbane District
Caboolture Station.
15th July 1930.

Relative to having the three children referred to in the attached report brought before the Children's Court at Caboolture on the 14th instant, in compliance with Inspector Farrell's minute on the attached reports.

Sir,

I beg to report in compliance with your minute on the attached report, I had the three children, Douglas Kearns, Mary Elizabeth Dalton and Nellie Ella Dalton brought before the Children's Court here on the 14th instant, before Mr G.E. Harwood, J.P. and Mr E. Kemp, J.P.

... [section not quoted or made visible on original copy above to keep matters private] ...

Evidence in support of the charge was given ... After hearing the evidence tendered I asked that these children be sent to the Aboriginal Home at Purga, Lizzie Kearns the mother stated that she had no objections to the children being sent to this home, as she was satisfied that it would be in their best interest to have them sent there.

The Bench then decided to have them sent to this Home until they attain the age of 18 years.

These children were conveyed to the Brisbane Watch House by Constable Devantier on the 14th instant together with warrants of detention duly signed by the adjudicating Justices for their detention at the Purga Aboriginal Home.

I issued the mother of the three children with a requisition to Brisbane for to enable her to catch the Boat to Bribie Island as there was no other mode of conveyance from here to her home at Toorbul Point. I did not issue her with a requisition for her return by boat from Brisbane, as she did not know when she would return to Bribie, arrangements were made for her at the Depot for her at Brisbane.

I have also made arrangements for her return at Toorbul Point when she arrives at Bribie.

(Sgd). T. J. Hogan,

A/Sergt.1051.a

The old people I write about in this story are gone now. Being raised by these old people in an extended family taught you the honesty and deepness of relationships. As I grew older and had earned the right to sit at the table, we would talk stories whilst sucking guppatea after guppatea. Each would contribute to tellin' stories; fragments of fragments would come together to be made whole. Aboriginal readers will see their own family members in this story for there is commonality, a tragic historical reality that every Aboriginal person has been impacted by the Stolen Generations. Laguna storyteller Leslie Silko (1997) says,

> They [stories] aren't just entertainment. Don't be fooled. They are all we have, you see. All we have to fight off illness and death. You don't have anything if you don't have stories.
>
> (p. 2)

I lean into bell hooks' (1990) theoretical insights of living and being in the margins as sites of radical possibility (p. 341). The story of three children being taken is a story I hold tenderly and in many respects, its theoretical underpinnings seem obvious. Acts of dispossession – from lands, from families, from self – to occupy the margin has been, and continues to be, a site of struggle, fear and terror, and sadness and pain. These sites, however, are not fixed locations, and Aboriginal agentic being has recast the margin time and time again.

The children I speak of, my old people, were not well educated in the schooling sense; however, their hunger for knowing was drawn of the world. As adults, recalling the lives of the child within, their analysis of power was astute. As incarcerated children and enslaved teenagers and young adults, those old people keenly observed the mechanisms of white supremacist power at close quarters. In reflective worldliness, those old people embodied resilience as a tool of self-determination, a tool to decolonise. In living, breathing, feeling and thinking about the margins, those old people, as with many other Aboriginal peoples, have come to claim this site as their own. I tell this story, standing in unison with the three so that this story is known. So that their lives matter. To claim voice in the margins.

### Principle: storying is embodied relational meaning making

> The body, through its states of arousal, awareness, and sensory experiences – such as listening to music, for instance, or hearing a loved one's voice or smelling a certain fragrance – has the ability to transport us elsewhere.
>
> (Pinkola Estes, 1992, p. 205)

Through embodied storying we can transport to the lived experience of others. As Walter Benjamin (1968/1999) wrote, "the storyteller takes what he tells from experience – his own or that reported by others. And he in turn makes it the experience of those who are listening to the tale" (p. 87). Storying evokes transportation into that moment – to weep, to yearn, to see, to hear, to pain, to taste, to love with the protagonists. Through such, stories can elucidate "powers of intuition, insight, sensory healing, and the rapture hidden in the body" (Pinkola Estes, p. 206). As Clarissa Pinkola Estes explains earlier, "the body is no dumb thing from which we struggle to free ourselves"; it is "a tangle of neurological umbilici to other worlds and experiences" (p. 205). Through embodied storying, we privilege sensation, emotion and spirit to actively create, interpret and decipher symbols as sensory beings through awakening, reclaiming and retaining memories that evoke joy, laughter, tears and thoughtfulness, and nurture our emotional, intellectual and spiritual selves.

Clarissa Pinkola Estes' (1992) sharing of La Mariposa, Butterfly woman, beautifully illustrates the power of embodied storying. It is her experience of witnessing a Hopi La Mariposa dance, "the wildest of the wild, a living numen" (p. 209) at Puyé, New Mexico. Anticipation for the Butterfly woman is built across pages with audience members' wild and beautiful imaginings. Those who are not familiar with La Mariposa are surprised by her age when she arrives.

> It is fitting that Wild Woman/Butterfly Woman is old and substantial, for she carries the thunderworld in one breast, the underworld in the other. Her back is the curve of the planet Earth with all its crops and foods and animals. The back of her neck carries the sunrise and sunset. Her left thigh holds all the lodgepoles, her right thigh all the she-wolves of the world. Her belly holds all the babies that will ever be born. Butterfly

woman is the female fertilizing force. Carrying the pollen from one place to another, she cross-fertilizes, just as the soul fertilizes mind with night-dreams, just as archetypes fertilize the mundane world. She is the center. She brings the opposites together by taking a little from here and putting it there. Transformation is no more complicated than that. This is what she teaches. This is how the butterfly does it. This is how the soul does it . . . She is shaking her feather fan, and she's hopping, for she is spilling spiritual pollen all over the people who are there . . . She is using her entire body as a blessing, her old frail, big, short-legged, short-necked, spotted body. This is woman connected to her wild nature, the translator of the instinctual, the fertilizing force, the mender, the rememberer of old ideas. She is La Voz Mitologica . . . The butterfly dancer must be old . . . because she is allowed to touch everyone: boys, babies, men, women, girl children, the old, the ill, and the dead.

(p. 211)

We acknowledge the Hopi peoples for their profound storying wisdom in the La Mariposa dance that we look to as a provocative illustration of embodied storying. Clarissa describes the woman's body who performs La Mariposa as storied, her body reflects place and her shaking, hopping and touching spread embodied storying to all present. The spread of pollen is the sprinkling of tiny seeds to spur thought, to spur identity work, to feed relations to others, to feed connection to place, to feed the soul.

Embodied storying, in turn, provokes relationality: to feel and know another. Story nurtures understanding of others. The complexities of humanity are not always visible in everyday interactions. Yet as Nussbaum (1997) claimed, the understandings of humanity can be reached via the training of the imagination that storytelling fosters. People in stories are imagined, then understood "as spacious and deep, with qualitative differences from oneself and hidden places worthy of respect" (p. 90). Storytelling cultivates a deeper understanding of difference that nurtures respect for others. Through the embodied relational meaning making of storying, complexities of humanity (such as perseverance and injustice) can be grasped, and understanding and compassion for others nurtured. To be compassionate, Nussbaum claims, requires "a sense of one's own vulnerability to misfortune" (p. 91) by imagining that this suffering could be happening to you. This is what Nussbaum referred to as *sympathetic imagination*, and it requires "imaginative and emotional receptivity" and the demonstration of "a capacity for openness and responsiveness" (p. 98). Thus, we argue that embodied relationality of storying has profound capacity to nurture heartfelt understanding of another's position, another's lived experience, another's tragedy, another's joy and wonder.

## Louise stories

Here I offer an example of storying as embodied meaning making in written form. The piece is from sensory ethnographic research of the social practice arts project *The Walking Neighbourhood* (in which children lead walks of local neighbourhoods as public performance) in Chiang Mai, Thailand. To heighten the connection to embodiment, I draw on animic ontology (Ingold, 2000, 2011), sensory ethnography (Pink, 2009) and agential realism (Barad, 2007, 2010, 2012). From Ingold, I understand animic ontology as a way of being within a complex network of reciprocal interdependence, sustained through perpetually drawing on the vitality of others. All forms are transient and ephemeral that "meet, merge and split apart again, each taking with them something of the other" (Ingold, 2000, p. 113). Barad's (2007) agential realism offers a mechanism to explain how matter meets, merges and splits apart again. Matter is understood as an active participant in the world that "is a dynamic intra-active becoming that never sits still" (p. 170). Agential realism's concept of "intra-actions" enables the reading of distinct entities, agencies and events emerging from actions, not on the preexistence of predetermined meanings of constructs. Agencies are only defined in relation to their reciprocal interconnection. This defining is enhanced through focussed attention to the sensorial, drawing from Pink's (2009) principles for sensory ethnography (perception, place, knowing, memory and imagination).

*With limited knowledge of Thai language, I let go of privileging meaning making through words and actively heightened my sensory awareness to make meaning through entwined visual, auditory, tactile, gestural and olfactory modes. I embrace openness to being "alive and open to a world in continuous birth" (Ingold, 2011, p. 64), engaging with the world as a source of astonishment. Such a way of being is curious and welcoming of the new and unknown. Through a more open (animic) and sensorial way of being, I endeavoured to welcome all that the Walking Neighbourhood child hosts wanted to share of the neighbourhoods of Old Chiang Mai. Allow me to take you on a walk with 6-year-old Seemie in Old Chiang Mai.*

*With a sparkling smile, Seemie, dressed in a pink dress topped with a crocheted white bolero and wide koala-shaped thongs, held her hand out to accompany me. I entered the walk with openness – letting go of preexisting conceptions of Seemie as child and me as adult, of me as foreigner (*farang*) and Seemie as a local; rather we were beings engaging with the streets of Old Chiang Mai. Seemie wrapped her hand in mine to take me on the walk.*

*I felt the delicate nature of Seemie's small hand in mine. My senses alerted to the weight, texture and warmth of her hand, that is neither a subject (i.e., to be used for a purpose, e.g., to guide me in direction of the walk) nor an object of observation. I sensed a "proximity of otherness that brings the other nearly as close as oneself. Perhaps closer . . . an infinity of others – other beings, other spaces, other times" (Barad, 2012, p. 206). Her hand is matter intertwined with the matter of my hand, engaged in the intra-activity of handholding. The affect of connection to another is created. My embodiment was integrally entangled with Seemie's. I attended to the wave of sensations: warmth, softness, tenderness and delicacy. In that moment of my hand being taken in Seemie's I had an ethico-onto-epistemological awakening that opened corporeal awareness of connectivity and entanglement: entanglement of alterity, generations, of child and adult, of interculturalism.*

*Seemie was leading the walk; she was responsible for me. Or as an adult, does the default for responsibility always defer to me? In agential realism, I am embodied, I am with Seemie, I am not an outsider observing in, I am in the moment with Seemie, I am engaged in walking along streets of Old Chiang Mai with Seemie. I am adult and child at the same time; binaries blur.*

*Our only shared words were greetings (*sawatdee-ka*) and gratitude (*korp-kun-ka*). By not sharing a language, the emphasis on words diminished; materiality and performativity claimed more space. My senses heightened to the new urban landscape. All I knew from an adult's explanation before we set off on the walk was that Seemie was taking us to a mermaid house. Fresh to a foreign city with sensory ethnographic sensibilities, I existed in the indeterminacy of quantum causality at the heart of Barad's (2007, 2010) concept of intra-actions. With openness to instability and impossibility, I searched for some threads of stability and possibility in my sensory memories – for balance, for meaning. A mermaid house – what could that be? I imagined what a mermaid house might be. A museum where Thai folklore of mermaids was stored and documented? Was it someone's home inspired in design by mermaids? A building with a mermaid painted on it? Being in touch with more-than-human imaginings in intercultural folklore – images of half-fish, half-human beings across cultures floated in and out of my mind as Seemie led us onwards.*

*As we walked down narrow footpaths frequently obstructed by obstacles, such as electricity poles, trees and rubbish, I wanted to engage with Seemie to make conversation, such as "How much further?" "Where is the mermaid house?" I guess driven by previous patterns of walking with another, you converse. Without Thai, all I could do was point and Seemie smiled and nodded. Committed to holding my hand, Seemie led the way. With the anticipation of the unknown and unfamiliar and the rising temperature and humidity, sweat slipped between our hands, yet Seemie continued to carefully attend to holding my hand. Beads of sweat developed on her petite forehead.*

*Touching, sensing, is what matter does, or rather, what matter is: matter is condensations of response-ability. Touching is a matter of*

> response. Each of "us" is constituted in response-ability. Each of "us"
> is constituted as responsible for the other, as the other.
>
> *(Barad, 2012, p. 215)*

*I felt for Seemie and her commitment to being responsible for me and the group. She was diligently committed to holding my hand and leading the walk to her desired mermaid house. I wondered if she was perspiring from the heat alone or whether she anxious about leading the walk and having responsibility for a* farang. *She continued to smile sweetly at me and carefully hold my hand.*

*The entire group of 11 followed Seemie's lead. I had no idea where we were going, yet was comfortable in the adventure of being led to the unknown by a young child. Well, aside from the prickly discomfort of the heat. We crossed the road and turned into another road where Seemie stopped across from a carpentry workshop, let go of my hand to approach the translator, Kimmim, and spoke in Thai, which Kimmim, relayed as "It's not there!"*

*An agential cut, the indeterminate phenomena of the mermaid house became determined through local causal structure (Barad, 2007). Though determined as absent – as missing! Our willing curiosity to see the mermaid house was stumped. Could this, what appeared to be a manufacturing workshop, have been differently materialised as a mermaid house at another point in time? Spacetimemattering – that is, the differential patterns of mattering across different times and spaces (Barad, 2010) –rearticulated this workshop as the mistaken mermaid house. A few of us took photos to archive this puzzle.*

*I responded with empathy to Seemie's disappointment, through a convivial offer of a grimace. She shyly smiled, seemingly unfazed by not locating her mermaid house. The workshop to which Seemie had led us had a panel near the roof, with a shadowed mark suggesting a previously adhered decorative piece, but it was dirty and well-worn and looked like a well-established workshop for construction. It was puzzling that it could have changed from a young girl's perception of a mermaid house within 2 days, when she located the mermaid house as a destination for her hosted walk. The accompanying translator and Australian arts worker (Nathan) talked about what to do. Nathan suggested they talk about it at the group debrief on return.*

*Sai then led the group onto his destination. Seemie retrieved a camera from her cloth shoulder bag. We then shared intra-activity between human and nonhuman apparatuses (i.e., cameras). This became our new way of being, a shift from the physical connection of handholding to sharing visions of interest. Seemie photographed lotus flowers in a decorative pond on the footpath, sparkly signs, gates, flowers . . . flowers and more flowers all within two blocks. I focussed on visual data with a view to glean insight into Seemie's interests, to know her connections with matter in public spaces. I*

*photographed her aiming her camera at matter, noticing her connections*
*with places.*

*I regarded matter that I would have otherwise passed. Seemie taking*
*photos of matter in the urban environment physicalised her connection to*
*the neighbourhood, and my taking photos of Seemie connecting to matter*
*drew me in as another thread in a web of entangled connections, so that*
*we become with the data (Hultman & Lenz Taguchi, 2010, p. 534). I visu-*
*ally honoured with Seemie what she deemed worthy of archiving. Then we*
*crossed the road and turned up a narrow road and Seemie suddenly stopped.*
*I saw her looking at a large copper mermaid painting on a black wall behind*
*a gate. "Is this the mermaid house?" I asked, and she nodded affirmatively.*

*The open arms and curving body of the mermaid were alluring. Seemie*
*smiled delightedly, yet she dutifully did not pass the gate. Seemie knew the*
*boundaries of space; even the tantalising enticement of her object of desire*
*(the mermaid) did not intercept her compliance with the public/private*
*space divide. (This story is an adapted excerpt from Phillips, L. G. [2016].)*

Our storying in this book is limited to the two-dimensional form of words
on pages, with a sprinkling of images. To emphasise embodiment and
relationality in this principle, stories of dance, touch and sensation were
selected. Yet in the flesh, in the intimacy of teller and listener in the same
space, embodied storying is penetratingly felt, not through words, but
through bodies communicating with bodies, by a look in a teller's eye, the
subtlety of a nod, infectious laughter or the enticement of raised eyebrows.
We argue, no matter what mode storying takes, embodiment and relationality are central and not just for the hell of it, but because together they actually work to produce deeper understanding of phenomena.

## Principle: storying intersects the past and present as living oral archives

When we connect to stories of the past, we embody them, gifting past and
present together to give meaning today. Storying feeds embodied connection to world views. "Embodied storying is the active and continual, flesh
and bone practising of stories – as both tellings and theorizing – that shows
the production of cultures, identities, histories and rhetorics" (Cobos, 2012,
p. 23). Stories aren't just for the mind. They are theories to feed and nourish
the whole of being. They are created and received through whole-of-body
meaning making. Storying is about walking with others. There is no clinical
scientific distance. Rather, we are emplaced and embodied in lived stories
regardless of time. As researchers, we are integrated perceptual beings with
others, who honour the intimate sharing of matters, such as love and hate,
affect, aesthetics and spirituality, that are vehemently outcast in positivist

research (Clandinin & Rosiek, 2007, p. 44). The quality of storying is indicated through the potency of the storying to arouse vivid sensorial imaginings of lived experience (Denzin, 1997).

In Chapter 2 we have told ancestral stories, melding our family oral herstories with archival research. Storying research through this technique is a potent connection of intersecting past and present in creating new archives, new stories to tell and document.

## Tracey stories: "This Young Boy"

I share a further story. This time, of the young boy who stood in the Department of Native Affairs with his mother awaiting permission to travel from the authorities. In coming to first know this story I knew I had been given a gift with the words leaving the mouth of the storyteller, floating in space and falling onto my skin and into the heart and soul – fuel for the spirit. The act of telling, receiving, keeping, remembering and telling again is the essence of one life giving purpose to the other. It is a constant and invisible resuscitation of life that gives purpose to the generations that follow. It is a story of being at one with the present in the past.

*I see this young boy in my mind's eye. Maybe he is 10 – maybe a little older, maybe a little younger. It is hard to tell. He is bony and barefoot. His clothes mark him as poor. A slight sheen of pale-coloured dust covers the exposed skin of his legs and arms. His dark hair masses in loose curls on the top of his head and some cascade towards the centre of his forehead. With his head bent slightly forward, these locks of hair shield his eyes and allow him to survey his surrounds without being seen. He digs at the ground, alternating the rhythm with the large toes. It is not a desperate digging, just slow and deliberate. It gives the boy time to contemplate. Through his curls he sees the white-painted wood home; the shed, bigger than the house; fenced paddocks; and open land. He takes in the clusters of gums, the rise of the land in the distance, the dams on the flat, and contours of crumbling sandstone that once held the creek flows. It is a warm sun that shines down on him, but he knows that he will be sweating before the day is finished.*

*A white man appears at the fence in front of the shed. A lined face makes him older than he actually is. Brown leather straps are in his hand. He motions the boy towards him with his free hand and calls out, "Boy". "Boy" is not his name but he hears white people call him this all the time. The young boy takes up a canter and moves easily across the dirt towards the white man who calls. His muscle movements give up a slight hint of the man-body yet to come. He stops short of the white man with the leather straps in his hand. Without another word, the white man turns and walks toward the plough in the paddock. The boy, also silent, follows. They crouch*

*under the top rail of the fence and negotiate the gap to step into the pad-*
*dock. The white man pulls up at the plough and fixes the leather straps to*
*it. He works quickly. The boy watches and knows that the white man has*
*done this many times before. The white man again calls "Boy". The young*
*boy steps closer. The white man grips a shoulder of the young boy and man-*
*ages his body to turn. The young boy is now facing the other direction and*
*stands still whilst the white man positions the straps over his shoulder and*
*around his body. The young boy feels the weight of the white man through*
*the plough, through the leather straps. The white man tugs the straps whilst*
*simultaneously calling the boy to motion. The straps slap the back of his*
*shoulders.*

*This young boy of 10 – maybe a little younger, maybe a little older – grits*
*his teeth. An unfathomable anger takes hold of his bony body and it sets*
*his jaw tight. In the moment that it takes him to discard the straps and step*
*away from the plough, he has turned and looked at the white man – hard*
*and deliberate. His eyes burn a fierce indignation that catches the white*
*man off guard. This child will not plough this paddock today or any other*
*day. He walks away, the calling of "Boy! Boy!" becoming fainter with each*
*step. It was not the boy's first act of resistance and would not be his last.*

How are we to read this story? The story of the young boy informs
Aboriginal senses of sovereignty that are found in having identification
with country, a land to come from, a place to stand on, a standpoint position
(Haraway, 1991). An Aboriginal standpoint epistemology, derived from
standing on and in country, embodies stories across the generations to pre-
serve and protect Aboriginal sovereignty. Remembering the stories of previous generations, engaging in resistances to power that seek to subordinate,
developing an art for survival and resilience, looking at and learning about
colonisation in all its forms constitute a theoretical life. The theorising of
our lives through storying provides part of the impulse for the way in which
I wrote my thesis and write this book.

There is in storying an unravelling of the complex space where we, as
Aboriginal peoples, stand alone or with other Aboriginal peoples and hold
to a hope that white systems, ideologies and individuals offer possibilities
for liberation. The historical and contemporary experience of subjugation,
denial and indifference tells a different story. A story difficult to shake, to
disrupt. My storying is not meant to stand for all of Aboriginal Australia.
Too much homogenization of our Aboriginal being has already occurred.
Storying told by Aboriginal peoples speaks of experiences of whiteness for
the ways in which it has sought to construct us. It is a collection of stories
that document our cultural and intellectual warriorship (Moreton-Robinson,
2000) in these white spaces and in these times, whilst acknowledging the
cultural and Aboriginal knowledge legacies given to us by of our old people
for coping.

This story is now a generation removed from the Aboriginal warrior boy child. I keep this story close to me; it is a story of a life lived, rarely voiced. It is a gift given. It is fuel for the spirit. In the act of telling, receiving, keeping, remembering and telling again, it is the essence of one life giving purpose to the other. It is a constant and silent act of resuscitation of a life, giving purpose to the generations that follow. In its totality, it is a story of heartbreaking sadness, of unexplainable inhumanity, and of struggle that heralds a celebration for survival. It is a story similar to the many stories given to us by our old people who lived in the racialised spaces and times before us.

### Principle: storying enacts collective ownership and authorship

Storying is a collective process. Stories are collectively created and collectively interpreted. The knowledge in a story is not owned by one, but many. There is no one author, but authors.

Stories resist the ravages of time. Aboriginal Australians are the greatest custodians of stories to have ever walked this planet, recalling the longest oral histories (Cane, 2013). Stories of giant marsupials aren't fantasy – they are lived experiences of coexisting with megafauna, passed down generation after generation. Stories are experiences "passed from mouth to mouth . . . from the speech of many nameless storytellers" (Benjamin, 1968/1999, p. 84). Across history, across cultures, across the world, artisans and travellers have shared stories with those they have met, travelling from home to home, village to village, group to group. European women in particular would gather to spin and weave and make baskets and clothing, exchanging tales of their lives and others (Haase, 2008). As Benjamin described, stories claim places in the memory of the listener, so that it becomes integrated into their own experience, so then they are inclined to repeat it to someone else. Stories passed on from one to another accumulate traces of each storyteller: "traces of the storyteller cling to the story the way the handprints of the potter cling to the clay vessel" (Benjamin, 1968/1999, p. 91). There is no one author but many, with each storyteller's world views and lived experiences shining through. "Storytellers tend to begin their story with a presentation of the circumstances in which they themselves have learned what is to follow" (Benjamin, p. 91). The context/circumstance of coming to know the story locates and roots the knowing.

Yet academia heralds the works of individual scholars – especially white male scholars – so that adulation is widespread. The Foucault fan club, Bourdieu fan club, Deleuze fan club and so on – academic idolation of these white male scholars is widespread and disturbing. Collective ownership and authoring of storying counters the privileging of individual authorship in academia, and foregrounds place and the value of Aboriginal story in country. We do recognise that many white male scholars offer insight into phenomena, though we argue for equitable sourcing of wisdom, and we hope you have recognised throughout the book that we have looked to Aboriginal and white, female and male, global north and global south wisdom. Here · in this moment, to enhance the point of foregrounding place, we do so in acknowledgement of connection to country in Aboriginal wisdom. We do this as an antidote to Doreen Massey and Pat Jess' (1995) caution of the placelessness of modern western society and in appreciation of Jacques Derrida's (1991) epitome: "Cinders there are: Place there is" (p. 37): beings come and transpire, but place remains. We foregrounded our relations to country/place in the opening of this storying book, and each story that we have shared we have commenced by locating the story.

Publishers demand author names, and promotions committees and grant applications demand an individual's list of publications. How to reconcile collective ownership and authoring in academia is problematic, though coauthored papers are common. Six seems to be the acceptable maximum, with referencing styles such as APA (American Psychological Association) substituting *et al.* for all authors listed past the sixth name, always privileging the first in this competitive space. Academic portfolios demand the percentage input for coauthored publications. How can such be measured? Of course, you may consider the proportion of how much you wrote, but that is honouring the written form of authoring alone. Some author more through ideas and through spoken words, some through imagery, some through song and so on.

We recognise that academia is a much larger beast than a dynamic duo espousing the wonders of storying. We are pressured to assert individual authorship (especially in the tenuous position as an early career academic) to develop a "track record" – to prove national and international recognition. However, there are ways to foreground the collective voice. Here are a few that we have located in the development of this book. Those who are asserting the collective voice in academia are in the main women and feminists. As noted by Haraway (1991) in Chapter 1, "we [feminists] do need an earth-wide network of connections, including the ability partially to translate knowledges among very different – power-differentiated – communities" (p. 187). Collectives provide networked connections and are a mechanism for women to resist the whiteness and maleness of neoliberal academia.

Some of the examples of collective authorship that stand apart from group authoring (a.k.a. et al.) include J. K. Gibson-Graham, the Res-Sisters, the Great Lakes Feminist Geography Collective, and the Women Who Write Collective. J. K. Gibson-Graham is the morphed pen name of two academics in human geography – Julie Graham and Katherine Gibson – formed in

1992 (Rose, 2013, n.p.). Their collective authorship through J. K. Gibson-Graham commenced in 1996 with their first book, *The End of Capitalism As We Knew It*. They continued to write and publish as the collective pen name for 14 years, until sadly, Julie Graham passed away suddenly in 2010. J. K. Gibson-Graham continues to publish, as Katherine Gibson still feels that many of the things she is thinking and talking about are in conversation with Julie (Gibson & Rose, 2013, n.p.). The Res-Sisters are a recently formed feminist collective of early career academics in the United Kingdom in the fields of sociology and cultural studies of education and youth. They aim to challenge inequality in (and out of) academia, to resist the neoliberal agenda and to make space for alternative voices to be heard (Res-Sisters, n.d.). Their name reflects their "shared occupational and political identities: as feminist academics engaged in and committed to research, resistance and sisterhood" (The Res-Sisters, 2017, pp. 268–269). The Res-Sisters collectively author as a political act of resistance to "the hyper-individualised and competitive modes of working that academia encourages" (p. 269). In following collective principles of distributive leadership, there is no "lead author". Instead, they all contribute through discussion, writing and editing, acknowledging that different members have different capacities to contribute at different times. The collective of nine holds space for locating agreement and differences, for spurring ideas that bounce of each other and even for completing each other's sentences. What is central to their practice is kindness – a much-needed antithesis to the cold, harsh conditions of competitive individualism in academia.

There are other feminist academic collectives emerging across the globe. The Great Lakes Feminist Geography Collective foregrounds slowness for "both a commitment to good scholarship and a feminist politics of resistance to the accelerated timelines of the neoliberal university" (Mountz et al., 2015, p. 1238). They too emphasise care and kindness. In their storying, at first individual stories of isolation are shared. Then they move to "a more collective form of response and action" from "experiences that cut across multiple trajectories representing different times in our lives" (p. 1239). Slow scholarship as collective action, they argue, "enables a feminist ethics of care that allows us to claim some time as our own, build shared time into everyday life, and help buffer each other from unrealistic and counterproductive norms that have become standard expectations" (pp. 1253–1254). In this space, knowledge production is conducted with care.

The Women Who Write Collective, a group of female academics based in Australia in the fields of education and the creative industries, also foregrounds an ethics of care and look to like-minded groups, people and places of connection and belonging, for sustenance, nourishment and energy (The Women Who Write, n.d.). They have purposefully chosen to write, share and coexist among collective stories. They liken their practice of collectively authoring to the bird practice of flying in a V formation. This flying formation is learned from observing and responding to each other, with frequent shifts in who is leading at the apex, and through collaboration, cooperation and relationship, endurance for long hauls is enabled (Black, Crimmins, & Jones, 2017).

These are examples of academics purposefully choosing to collectively author, though what we argue is that storying enacts collective authorship, and ownership of storying defies individual authorship. We see that place and others have their hands all over each story. It is arrogant and selfish to claim a story to one name. In our own storying work, we weave collective authors into the storying so that their presence is felt. As storytellers, we set the scene for the stories – where we were, who we were with, what provoked the knowing. Country and place owns/holds the story, rather than people.

## Tracey stories

> In fact, one aspect of the Indigenous worldview is that it takes a thousand voices to tell a story.
>
> (Wilshire, 2006, p. 160)

I led a small research project in 2012–2013. The project aimed to tell stories about teaching from the perspective of initial teacher education students, classroom teachers and academics. Setting aside the inflexibilities of a project – grant application writing and accounting, meeting milestones, producing research outcomes, writing publications, managing budgets and so forth – there was belly laughing, fussing, tellin' stories in stories that meant talking over one another . . . loudly, more laughing, seriousness, shame-job moments, heads together solving issues, bucketloads of pride and celebration. It wasn't a thousand voices, though on some days it felt like this. This was a majority-Aboriginal project from myself as the leader, to the producer, camera operators (some of our Aboriginal media students) and research participants (some of our teacher education students and a few of our academic staff). The synergies of our own kinship systems easily melded into our working relationships, emphasising respect, sharing knowledge, listening to knowledge holders and caring for each other. Our Aboriginal world views were in research action and it was a deadly story.

## Louise stories

To illustrate how storying enacts collective ownership and authorship, I share with you a brief vignette from research with the project *Walking Borders:*

*Arts Activism for Refugee and Asylum Seeker Rights* (http://walkingbor
ders.net). The work was initiated by arts activist Scotia Monkivitch and supported by many other artists and activists. The storied vignette that follows is
an excerpt from an article coauthored with Cate Montes. Cate and I walked
the borders with Scotia and many others, and composed storied vignettes in
the article through merging self-storied journalling with stories we heard from
Scotia and other participating arts activists. The stories had no one author, but
many. Here, we collectively story the power of the motif of the paper boat, to
provoke reflection on asylum-seeker politics in Australia:

> A woman waiting for a bus glanced down and, on noticing the deli-
> cate boat at her feet, wept. The delicate little boats provided a stark
> contrast to the policing harshness of authoritarian blue, impenetrable
> fencing, and the constant alarming hum of helicopters; they softened
> the edges. Though Walking Borders spoke out against the violation of
> asylum seekers, it seemed that approaching this from a point of quiet-
> ness and beauty offered an alternative provocation for attention to the
> dissensus. Through aesthetics of the political dimension, the paper boat
> communicated fragility, the line – unrelenting repetition . . . a trace of
> political poetics. The ephemeral nature of the work added to the aes-
> thetics: the transience of the provocation – to be felt – not to be grasped
> or recorded.
>
> (Phillips & Montes, 2017, p. 8)

*Figure 3.1* Walking Borders paper boats aligning security fencing at the G20 Summit,
Brisbane.

Photograph taken by Scotia Monkivitch; permission to reproduce granted.

We acknowledge the contributors to the stories throughout the article by quoting participants and explicitly noting that the vignettes are co-storied. In this case, key contributors to the stories were happy to be named in the published article, but there are times when contributors to stories choose not to be named, or are no longer with us. In these moments, I take my role as guardian for the collective story seriously, and consider carefully the position of the silent, unnamed author and place myself in their shoes and ask, "Would I want this story in the public eye?" and if so, "What do I want to have heard?" Ethical questions are ever present in the collective ownership and authorship of storying.

## Together/two-gather

In sum, we offer these five principles as a conversation starter in the work of research through, with and as storying. Those of you who story may agree, dispute and add to these principles. We hope those of you who are fresh to storying may see these principles and illustrative examples as offering guidance to your emergent practice.

## References

Ahmed, S. (2014). *Willful subjects*. London: Duke University Press.
Anzaldúa, G. (1990). Haciendo caras, una entrada. In G. Anzaldúa (Ed.), *Making face, making soul: Creative and critical perspectives by feminists of color* (pp. xv–xxviii). San Francisco, CA: Aunt Lute Books.
Archibald, J. A. (2008). *Indigenous storywork: Educating the heart, mind, body, and spirit*. Vancouver: UBC Press.
Arendt, H. (1970). *Men in dark times*. London: Cape.
Arendt, H. (1998). *The human condition* (2nd ed.). Chicago: The University of Chicago Press (Original work published 1958).
Barad, K. (2007). *Meeting the universe halfway: Quantum physics and the entanglement of matter and meaning*. Durham: Duke University Press.
Barad, K. (2010). Quantum entanglements and hauntological relations of inheritance: Dis/continuities, spacetime enfoldings, and justice-to-come. *Derrida Today*, 3(2), 240–268.
Barad, K. (2012). On touching: The inhuman that therefore I am. *Differences: A Journal of Feminist Cultural Studies*, 23(3), 206–223.
Barone, T. (1995). Persuasive writings, vigilant readings, and reconstructed characters: The paradox of trust in educational storytelling. *Qualitative Studies in Education*, 8(1), 63–74.
Benjamin, W. (1999). *Illuminations* (H. Zorn, Trans.). London: Pimlico (Original English version published 1968).
Berger, R. J., & Quinney, R. (2005). The narrative turn in social inquiry. In R. J. Berger & R. Quinney (Eds.), *Storytelling sociology: Narrative as social inquiry* (pp. 1–11). Boulder, CO: Lynne Rienner Publishers.

Black, A. L., Crimmins, G., & Jones, J. K. (2017). Reducing the drag: Creating V formations through slow scholarship and story. In S. Riddle, M. Harmes, & P. A. Danaher (Eds.), *Producing pleasure in the contemporary university* (pp. 137–156). Rotterdam, The Netherlands: Sense Publishing.

Cane, S. (2013). *First footprints: The epic story of the first Australians*. Crows Nest, NSW: Allen & Unwin.

Chawla, D. (2011). Between stories and theories: Embodiments, disembodiments, and other struggles. In D. Chawla & A. Rodriguez (Eds.), *Liminal traces: Storying, performing, and embodying postcoloniality* (pp. 13–24). Rotterdam, The Netherlands: Sense Publishers.

Clandinin, D. J., & Rosiek, J. (2007). Mapping a landscape of narrative inquiry: Borderland spaces and tensions. In D. J. Clandinin (Ed.), *Handbook of narrative inquiry: Mapping a methodology* (pp. 35–76). Thousand Oaks, CA: Sage.

Cobos, C. C. (2012). *Embodied storying, A methodology for Chican@ rhetorics: (Re)making stories, (un)mapping the lines, and re-membering bodies* (Doctoral thesis). Texas A&M University, USA.

Coles, R. (1989). *The call of stories: Teaching and the moral imagination*. Boston: Houghton Mifflin.

Delgado, R. (1989). Storytelling for oppositionists and others: A plea for narrative. *Michigan Law Review, 87*, 2411–2441.

Denzin, N. K. (1997). *Interpretive ethnography: Ethnographic practices for the 21st century*. Thousand Oaks, CA: Sage.

Derrida, J. (1991). *Cinders* (N. Lukacher, Trans.). Lincoln: University of Nebraska Press.

Duncan, M. C. (1998). Stories we tell ourselves about ourselves. *Sociology of Sport Journal, 15*, 95–108.

Environmental Humanities. (2013). *Take back the economy: An interview with Katherine Gibson* [Video File]. Retrieved from www.youtube.com/watch?v=gJHA dzye4hw

Estes, C. P. (1992). *Women who run with the wolves: Contacting the power of the wild woman*. London: Rider.

Fisher, W. R. (1987). *Human communication as narration*. Columbia: University of South Carolina Press.

Gibson-Graham, J. K. (1996). *The end of capitalism (as we knew it): A feminist critique of political economy*. Oxford, UK: Blackwell Publishers.

Glassie, H. H. (1993). *Irish folktales* (New ed.). London: Penguin.

Haase, D. (2008). *The Greenwood encyclopaedia of folktales and fairy tales*. Westport, CT: Greenwood Publishing Group.

Haraway, D. (1991). *Simians, cyborgs, and women*. New York: Routledge.

hooks, b. (1990). Marginality as a site of resistance. In R. Ferguson, M. Gever, T. T Minh-ha, & C. West (Eds.), *Out there: Marginalisation and contemporary cultures* (pp. 341–344). New York: New Museum of Contemporary Art.

Hultman, K., & Lenz Taguchi, H. (2010). Challenging anthropocentric analysis of visual data: A relational materialist methodological approach to educational research. *International Journal of Qualitative Studies in Education, 23*(5), 525–542.

Ikemoto, L. (1997). Furthering the inquiry: Race, class, and culture in the forced medical treatment of pregnant women. In A. K. Wing (Ed.), *Critical race feminism: A reader* (pp. 136–143). New York: New York University Press.

Ingold, T. (2000). *The perception of the environment: Essays on livelihood, dwelling and skill.* London: Routledge.

Ingold, T. (2011). *Being alive: Essays on movement, knowledge and description.* New York: Routledge.

Jeffers, S. (1987). *Feel the fear and do it anyway.* London: Century.

Kwaymullina, A. (2015). *Let the stories in: On power, privilege and being an Indigenous writer.* Retrieved from www.wheelercentre.com/notes/let-the-stories-in-on-power-privilege-and-being-an-indigenous-writer

Ladson-Billings, G. (1998). Just what is critical race theory and what's it doing in a nice field like education. In L. Parker, D. Deyhele, & S. Villenas (Eds.), *Race is . . . race isn't: Critical race theory and qualitative studies in education* (pp. 7–30). Boulder, CO: Westview Press.

Lawson, R. (1995). Critical race theory as praxis: A view from outside to the outside. *Howard Law Journal, 38,* 353–370.

Lyotard, J. F. (1984). *The postmodern condition: A report on knowledge* (G. Bennington & B. Massumi, Trans.). Manchester, UK: Manchester University Press.

Massey, D., & Jess, P. M. (Eds.). (1995). *A place in the world?: Places, cultures and globalization.* Oxford: Oxford University Press in association with Open University.

Moreton-Robinson, A. (2000). *Talkin' up to the white woman: Indigenous women and feminism.* St Lucia, Qld: University of Queensland Press.

Mountz, A., Bonds, A., Mansfield, B., Lloyd, J., Hyndman, J., Walton-Roberts, M., . . . Curran, W. (2015). For slow scholarship: A feminist politics of resistance through collective action in the neoliberal university. *ACME: An International Journal for Critical Geographies, 14*(4), 1235–1259.

Nussbaum, M. C. (1997). *Cultivating humanity: A classical defense of reform in liberal education.* London: Harvard University Press.

Pink, S. (2009). *Doing sensory ethnography.* Thousand Oaks, CA: Sage.

Phillips, L. G. (2016). Walking in indeterminate spaces: Possibilities for political coexistence. *Qualitative Research Journal, 16*(4). doi:10.1108/QRJ-09-2015-0084

Phillips, L. G., & Montes, C. (2017). Walking borders: Explorations of aesthetics in ephemeral arts activism for asylum seeker rights. *Space and Culture* (Advance online publication). doi:10.1177/1206331217729509

Quintero, E. P., & Rummel, M. K. (2015). *Storying: A path to our future: Artful thinking, learning, teaching, and research.* New York, NY: Peter Lang.

The Res-Sisters. (2017). 'I'm an early career feminist academic: Get me out of here?' Encountering and resisting the neoliberal academy. In R. Thwaites & A. Pressland (Eds.), *Being an early career feminist academic global perspectives, experiences and challenges* (pp. 267–284). London: Palgrave MacMillan.

The Res-Sisters. (n.d.). *Res-Sisters – About.* Retrieved from https://ressisters.word press.com/about/

Rose, D. [Professor Deborah Rose]. (2013). *Take back the economy an interview with Katherine Gibson* [Video file]. Retrieved from www.youtube.com/watch?v=g JHAdzye4hw

Scott, K., & Robinson, E. (2011). Voices Australia's Aboriginal and Canada's First Nations literatures. *CLCWeb: Comparative Literature and Culture*, *13*(2). doi:10.7771/1481-4374.1747

Silko, L. (1997). *Ceremony*. New York: Viking Press.

Solórzano, D. G., & Yosso, T. J. (2001). Critical race and LatCrit theory and method: Counter-storytelling. *Qualitative Studies in Education*, *14*(4), 471–495.

Solórzano, D. G., & Yosso, T. J. (2002). Critical race methodology: Counter-storytelling as an analytical framework for education research. *Qualitative Inquiry*, *8*(1), 23–44.

Wallace, K. K. (2009). *Listen deeply, Let these stories in*. Alice Springs: Institute of Aboriginal Development Press.

Watson, I., Allon, F., Nicoll, F., & Neilson, B. (Eds.). (2002). On what grounds? Sovereignties, territorialities and Indigenous rights. *Borderlands E-Journal*, *1*(2). Retrieved from www.borderlands.net.au/vol1no2_2002/watson_laws.html

Wilshire, B. (2006). On the very ideas of a 'worldview' and of 'alternative world-views'. In F. A. Jacobs (Ed.), *Unlearning the language of conquest: Scholars expose anti-Indianism in America* (pp. 160–272). Austin: University of Texas Press.

The Women Who Write. (n.d.). *We are 'the women who write'*. Retrieved from www.thewomenwhowrite.com/about.html

Young-Bruehl, E. (1977). Hannah Arendt's storytelling. *Social Research*, *44*(1), 183–190.

# 4    Storying ways

Storying is emergent and responsive, so it is not possible, nor is it line with the essence of the liveliness of storying, to prescribe a process. What we offer here instead are conversational reflections on how we story. To frame this conversation on process, we talked over lunch, mulling over what the questions we are interested in when coming to understand more about our practice are. And over time we identified a series of questions to ask each other. Before any research is considered, we recognised that we need to consider the integrity of our work, so first we asked questions of ethics – who are we in storying and how do we engage with others? Then we looked to origins, asking, where do your stories come from? But it is not just the origins that matter, but rather how we hear (how do we really hear what matters) the stories that we need to hear from the people and places we go to locate stories. From the stories that we gathered through emergent and immersed listening, we then asked, how do you bring stories to life? We reflected on how we storied together all the stories that we heard to make them alive for others to feel. And finally, we talked about stories as gifts: how are stories gifted?

## Ethics: which way?

The question of which way is more than a directional request. The first time Tracey heard this speaking was when she was with members of the Torres Strait Islander community, and since that time, whenever she is in the presence of Torres Strait Islander individuals, she hears these words as a first point of conversation. The words are at once a greeting but simultaneously ask questions, from speaker to listener, of where have you been, what for, what are you/we doing, how and why and when? We borrow this phrasing, as there is an essence of research framing in the intent of the words. We lean into its multiple-questioning technique to think through our positionalities as Aboriginal and white researchers and our intersubjective relationships

DOI: 10.4324/9781315109190-4

with both Aboriginal communities for conducting research and for the storying of research.

## *Tracey*

There are many issues that need to be addressed within Aboriginal communities – matters of health, education, housing, legal matters, preservation of languages, Indigenous knowledge systems and so on. All are critical to sustaining the well-being of Aboriginal peoples, societies and cultures, now and into the future. And the reality is that, as a consequence of colonisation and its devastating effect on our communities, there is an urgency to finding answers, appropriate responses and strategies for these matters. Surviving, recovering from and living through colonisation in its various assumptions and technologies has generated various responses. Certainly, Aboriginal responses may well be found within our own communities; however, we may need to look outside our communities for knowledge, support and expertise. Research can be helpful to the strengthening of our communities.

It is from my dual location of being an Aboriginal woman and being in the academy that I now write about the process of "doing" research with Aboriginal people with all of the satisfaction, troubling, messy tangling and transformational possibilities that this can bring. In part I borrow from my doctoral studies (2014) to inform this writing about what constitutes ethical research with Aboriginal communities. As I have previously pointed to, it is important to be mindful of how the historical context, alluding to the relations of power – signified in the question "*Who* gets to do research?" – has worked to exclude and devalue Aboriginal authoritative engagement in research. The production of knowledge about us occurs through research processes that have not / do not come from spaces that seriously consult us. I remain open to hopefulness in the momentum for change.

Colleagues will often approach me for advice regarding research within Aboriginal communities. This is as it should be. Gaining advice from Aboriginal peoples is a solid and respectful starting point for those who want to engage in Aboriginal research. It is the case too that these researchers will be white and well intentioned. Well-intentioned white researchers are enthusiastic about the possibilities that researching in Aboriginal communities offers. From this point onwards, the dialogue can often become tangled and messy. There are complexities inherent. These types of conversations known by Aboriginal peoples throughout the academy elucidate the white researcher–Aboriginal research conundrum to sometimes reveal misrepresentations, presumptions and misguidedness. The unspoken ways in which white patriarchy informs research, and compels researchers (in this situation, white researchers) to do and to educate, caution, protect and resist (as Aboriginal researchers and as members of Aboriginal communities do), is felt in the dialogue.

Many white researchers have little understanding of Aboriginal peoples' and communities' lived realities, and give little thought for how their not knowing is problematic for Aboriginal peoples. Research must be a tool which assists in the uplift of communities, truly committing to community development as defined by the community and not by an external force. Having relationalities of meaning with Aboriginal peoples is a necessary precondition for deep thinking, through the racialised space of research in this context and the power differentials that exist. In the presence of deep thinking and resultant demonstrations, white researchers are better informed and received when entering Aboriginal communities, and research engagements are strengthened to benefit Aboriginal communities.

Entering Aboriginal communities, even when an Aboriginal person, and even where there are families and friends, is to be mindful of the protocols for entry onto Aboriginal land. If these protocols are confounded, then there is the risk of big shame, of being *myall* ("ignorant" in Aboriginal vernacular), and devaluing important relational capacities in engagements from the outset. As Ngarrindjerri scholar Darryle Rigney (2010) asserts,

> Indigenous worldviews and knowledge systems have significant implications for ethics processes in universities . . . in the discourse of research ethics, the researcher is often positioned as "objective" and charged with the power and the knowledge to determine what should be researched and who could be "consulted" in Indigenous research projects. This is a problematic positioning, focussing on the rights of the individual rather than the collective.
>
> (p. 3)

It is worthwhile noting that as Aboriginal peoples, we are not without agency. This means we are not sitting around waiting for the white researcher to come and solve our issues. What becomes critical in the research and even in initial dialoguing are the genuine intentions to share power. A failure to share in ways that make it possible for Aboriginal peoples and communities to feel safe in research is a failure in research ethics. Power sharing, respect for community, showing generosity and operating with a sense of care add to relational and positional capacities within the terms of Aboriginal ways of knowing. Breaches of Aboriginal protocols will weaken the trust needed in the research relationship. It is critical that research with white people will not injure. As Smith (1999) reminds us, "The terms research and problem are closely linked. For many Indigenous communities, research itself is taken to mean problem – the continued construction of Indigenous people as the problem" (p. 91).

There are critical and proactive purposes in which Aboriginal people feel called, on behalf of our communities, to engage in conversations about research and to do research, often in efforts to solve white-created problems in which we struggle with regimes of past and present historical containment and control. There are serious questions formed and forming in the phrase *which way?* used to title this section. Such questions focus the ethical-epistemological tensions associated with white researchers in the Aboriginal community space. Hard conversations are, in some respects, inevitable. There are so few informed white researchers of Aboriginal epistemologies. White researchers do need to experience equivalent ethical struggles when undertaking research that seeks to engage Aboriginal communities, rather than the tendency to gain/create knowledge from and about Aboriginal social spaces. Given the seriousness and urgency of issues in Aboriginal communities, conversations can ill afford to be shallow or emotionally laborious for Aboriginal discussants. Deeply respectful listening about Aboriginal ways of knowing and being is critical for white researchers to try or find ways to understand and conform to Aboriginal ways of being, in relation to country and to the people of country. See also Fredericks (2007); Dudgeon, Kelly, and Walker (2010); Vivian, Jorgensen, Bell, Rigney, Cornell, and Hemming (2016); Martin (2010) and Rigney (2006) for further understandings of researching with, about and in Aboriginal communities and ethical practice.

### *Louise*

I am a white researcher who has spent years listening and learning and asking myself and coresearchers, "Which way?" though of course with not such exquisite provocative succinctness; rather, I've fumbled with redundant verboseness. Even in writing this section, I proposed the questions of "How do you attend to others in storying?" and "Who are you as a storying researcher?" Then Tracey proposed the beautiful simplicity (yet all-encompassing) of the question "Which way?" I am constantly blown away by this quality in Indigenous world views, to nail the essence of a phenomena with such precision.

My "which way?" storying is on my experience as a non-Indigenous academic leading the Australian investigation of an international research project on children's citizenship with an Aboriginal community. I offer this story to provide some transparency about my ethical questions, issues and dilemmas in storying with a community when an outsider. I share thinking and actions on decisions of "which way?" to enter community, to build relationships and to seek approval, and the ongoing ethical tensions between what is happening in community and institutional research agendas. Scientific research has a legacy of tyranny for colonised peoples across the globe. Aboriginal children have been part of the Aboriginal Australian experience of being overresearched, "without the permission, consultation, or involvement of Aboriginal people", "generating mistrust, animosity, and resistance" in communities (Martin, 2003, p. 203). Researching young children can, and often is, a colonising practice, through unequal power structures with adults determining what, how and who are researched, often subjectifying and oversimplifying children for adult knowledge gain (Cannella & Viruru, 2004). With grave concern and sensitivity to these human rights cautions, the methodology for a study on young Aboriginal children's civic action and learning foregrounded relationship building over research agendas. Acutely aware of my whiteness and outsider positioning, I was invited into the community by an Aboriginal colleague, Kerryn Moroney (a proud Luritja country woman) who had a 6-year-plus relationship with the childcare community as a mentor. We visited a couple of times to get to know each other, talking about the centre, community, early childhood education and the project. Kerryn and I referred to the project in terms of children having voice, rights and being active contributors to community. Supportive of the project, the director took Kerryn and I to the home of an Elder who was executive on the centre's committee, to talk about the study and her thoughts on the project. It was a very humbling experience to be welcomed into an Elder's home. I have never been to the homes of, say, principals of schools in which I have researched. I was struck by the intimacy and generosity of this encounter. The Elder agreed, on behalf of the community, to approve the study taking place. I understood that her decision was guided by the physical presence of the director and Kerryn standing beside me on this project.

Kerryn and I visited a few more times across a year to build relationships with educators and discuss what children's rights and citizenship means to them. I would have visited way more if they were closer, though the community is half a day's travel away. It wasn't until 15 months after I had first visited the community that we entered classrooms to spend time with children and seek their consent. To decolonise conventional research methodologies, in which the researcher must not influence the research context and participants are surveilled as specimens (Smith, 2012), we became involved in their everyday practices. Kerryn and I are both early childhood teachers, so we joined in the children's activities and co-played, building relationships and getting to know the children. We played with the children and took part in all the day's activities – playing inside and out, setting up equipment, comforting children, serving food, cleaning and settling children to sleep. We did everything the educators did. I understood this as a cultural value – if you are there you are responsible, you contribute. After a few days, we introduced the video camera – showing the children what it did and asking if they wanted to be filmed. With the use of the camera's built-in projector, we played footage back to the children at group time, gleaning their feedback and response. The children could see and comment on what we were doing. To nurture reciprocity, we did what they did – so they did what we did – cameras were shared with the children. Our notebooks were also shared – the children too wanting to make notes. We also had a university ethics committee–approved consent form with pictures of children decorating a box, a camera, video camera, an audio recorder and a hand writing, asking them to tick what they agreed to in data gathering of the project. But it was in their actions that they really communicated their consent and trust in our presence and the project. Such as running to hug us on arrival, and calling us both Aunty, inviting us to film their activities, and my most treasured moment, when one 4-year-old boy, who carried his small backpack of toys everywhere, chose me to look after it when he wanted to enter a spontaneous soccer game outside.

Our research design originally was for children to initiate and engage in three civic action projects (one class based, one centre based, one community based). For months Kerryn and I endeavoured to support civic-action projects taking place with the kindergarten group: through conversations with educators about what we observed and what issues could be explored further, through sharing Aboriginal children's literature as provocations, through community walks, through inviting the children to take pictures of what they don't like – what they feel uncomfortable about – to see if any of these may incite a project. And across 4 months there were multiple changes to the teaching team, with at least eight different educators. The constant rupture in the teaching team meant they were in survival mode with no space to be proactive. As Linda Tuhui Smith (2012) noted, the lived reality is that "Indigenous peoples are not in control and are subject to a continuing set of external conditions" (p. 206). We became acutely aware that the research agenda was not aligned with the community's pressing needs and reality, though they so wanted the children to engage in civic action. The constant barrage of crises demanded urgent attention. And what was more important was for us to show support and be there for community.

Kerryn and I talked for hours and hours, and we talked for hours with the director and pedagogical leader, and we read Indigenous and non-Indigenous female scholars to locate possibilities for making meaning with ethical and culturally sensitive sensibilities that did not add to the colonising project, but rather offered hope for justice to come.

With heartfelt sensitivity for the beautiful people of the community, we foregrounded relationship building over research agendas. To be with the children and community and to fully commit to ethical research, I drew from Barad (2007) and asked, "What is being made to matter here?" and "How does that mattering affect what is possible to do and think?"

Drawing from Smith's (2012) lived wisdom, we sought to decolonise our research by seeking to understand the colonising experience, valuing Aboriginal knowledges and ways of being, and questioning what we have to do to reframe knowledge and knowledge making. To do this, we sat and listened to Elders, to educators, to families, to children – hearing their stories of discrimination, of hurt, of illness, of loss, of struggles, of wins, of hilarious misadventures, of love for others and country. Through these stories and witnessing the children's actions, we came to know core values that guide Aboriginal knowledges and ways of being. We came to see that the children were initiating civic action projects on daily basis. To really see what citizenship meant to young children, we noticed how they negotiated coexistence with each other in the shared space of an early learning centre. We let go of adult assumptions, definitions and directions.

We shared videos of children's actions and the writing of the stories with children, educators and families, to hear their readings of what mattered – what was valued – and have foregrounded community value of readings of children's citizenship in the publications from the research. Across the ongoing years of this research, we have questioned how the knowledges of this community can reframe what citizenship is, and what it can be for children. From years of listening and letting go of a research agenda, and all prior identities and just simply being there with community, I have been gifted with profound wisdom that I carry like a fragile ancient egg, wrapping for protection in transit and carefully, consultatively and collectively choosing where and when to place in public. It takes time and it takes patience, and pushing back against institutional deadlines and time frames.

## Where do stories come from?

The question of "Where do stories come from?" purposefully has no ownership embedded. This is not simply a pragmatic location question, like "What is the source of your stories?" to trace data. Rather it is also an existential question that poses thinking about origins, like we asked of ourselves in locating self in place and ancestral storying in Chapter 2. Looking to the origins of where also brings in the how and the why. Our ethics, informed by "Which way?" very much informs each of our thinking to "Where do stories come from?" Our "Which way?" values and thinking informs our purpose (why) and our practices (how) for locating, gathering and responsibly caring for locating stories. We hope that our conversation offers a diverse range of thinking about the origins and sourcing of stories that provokes further thinking for other storyers.

### Tracey

If I think about where my stories come from, they come from that lived life of my family or my friends or my colleagues. And in the telling of stories, there's a responsibility that I have in listening, particularly when I have an intention to retell that story. I can't do that story a disservice. If it is that I am present in the space of telling stories, it will be because, in most instances, I have relationality to the storyteller. So, I must take the story, at the very least, and hopefully tell it with the same effect, even when I have placed my own touch onto it. In turn, when I share the same story with others, who have relationality with me, a rhythm forms from the sharing. I reiterate, the stories I tell are the stories of our life since colonisation. Aboriginal people love stories and love to laugh at the craziness of ourselves in situation with colonising circumstance and the craziness of whiteness. Paul Collis (2016), Barkindji scholar, writes the following:

> Other storytellers, moved between two worlds – between the Whitefullas world and our world. Those storytellers use Western ways and different languages and shape-forming techniques, making use and sometimes making fun of the Whitefullas as they performed, dancing and speaking their way through their observations. In doing so, they made comments upon those who tried to hold power over us Blackfullas. Sometimes, the storytellers acted out the voice and presence of a policeman, or some other person of authority. Those old storytellers never missed a trick. They'd only act the vagabond in the world whilst collecting their stories.

The stories of colonisation were born of necessity, to understand, to protect, to resist, to battle, to adapt, to not adapt, for compassion, for kindness and for loss. I recall being told a story about our mob telling stories about white people on the east coast. This story travelled across this land and reached northern Australia to Aboriginal people there long before white people did. In telling stories, we are making meaning for ourselves, to be able to be in this space, our land.

### Louise

In thinking about this question of where stories come from, I refer to my research with children. It's very much about this practice of being with the children and listening, not just with my ears, but with my heart, and my soul, and all my senses. I recognise that the children aren't necessarily going to verbalise a story, but that their stories are embodied and enacted in how they engage with the world. And the stories that I listen to and gather are about rewriting the public discourse about how children are perceived. I seek to share stories that challenge perceptions of children as innocent, as vulnerable, as incompetent. The stories are sourced and created through listening very carefully, and reflecting very carefully, and thinking over time. It requires a lot of mulling and thinking over time. I do a sketch of a story quite immediately and come back to it sometime later, with thinking from theory and literature. And here I don't just mean academic literature, but also literary literature and folklore literature. For example, in coming to understand my great-great-grandmother's convict experience, I read historical nonfiction of women sent to Van Diemen's Land. And since my love of story and storytelling commenced, I have looked to folk tales from around the world for their metaphoric and symbolic interpretation of life, the universe and everything. And so over time, the story gets more and more flesh added to it, slowly bringing it to life, with energy from multiple sources.

### Tracey

Since you've been talking/writing, I've been thinking further about that notion of "Where do these stories come from?" And if I'm naming this as our lived life within colonisation, I am acknowledging that these are the stories at the interface (Anzaldua,1990; Nakata, 2007). At the interface, the story that the dominant tell is the story that becomes the truth. And as researchers, we are aiming to take the stories of our mob and we work to disrupt, or make deeper, those understandings of children, of Aboriginal adults and of our communities. A story by the dominant has the potential for greater distribution and currency because it latches onto existing stories of so-called Aboriginal abnormalcy – the traces of which are left in the sinuous trails across the country. As I am writing, I am reminded of the dominant story of Aboriginal welfare dependency. This story has enormous power within the wider Australian society, and through telling a fragment of the broken-up story of my grandmother, it is evident that the source of welfarism within Aboriginal communities resides in the colonising ethos of control, income management and containment in the lives of the previous generations. Storytelling in Aboriginal communities was and is an oral practice, but today in the writing and in the theorising of our stories, we are countering dominant knowings, and this is a critical tactic for breathing, feeling and sustaining our humanity.

### Louise

My intent with storying is to craft deeper, richer, embodied sensorial, relational understandings of phenomena that invite readers/listeners to come to understand another position for those whose rights we advocate for.

The stories don't come from one source alone, to build these fully fleshed-out stories, but rather multiple, diverse, carefully selected sources gathered over time. For example, with my *grand*-mothering story in Chapter 2, that was pieced together over decades. I didn't grow up being told stories of our old people. As I explained earlier, I went searching once I was confronted by the question "Where do you come from?" And then it was about finding fragments and looking further to find more to try and get more of a context. Across the years I have been ever so slowly drip fed small portions of stories of ancestors from various relatives. And it's about piecing those together, not just to compose an individual's story, but an individual experience within broader social, cultural and political events and thinking. For white occupiers on stolen Aboriginal land, it's about knocking grand notions of white Australian heroes off their pedestals and ripping back the carpet and exposing all those insidious secrets.

### Tracey

And in putting those fragments together, the gift of storying helps us imagine a differing truth to fill the void where Aboriginal voices have not been invited, have been rendered silent. That's the gift that stories bring. And it rewrites that critique of storying research that it is not intellectual, creative but not scientific. In piecing together all of those fragments, you do need to know your herstory, where you are from, and the agency that can be brought to shifting power relations. Let us be honest; if as Aboriginal peoples we story this land, then whitefellas also need to show truth in speaking to the first research questions that asks, "If you are not of this land then where is it that you come from?" and "Who are your mob, your people?" Storying research makes visible a differing flesh – the theoretical muscle, blood and sinew coming from and attached to the storying bone. Speaking truth in Aboriginal ways of knowing is a much more respected positionality and the sharing of story, in research and other spaces, shifts the paradigmatic tendencies of whiteness away from control and containment towards a kinder, new story for freedom, compassion and justice.

## How do we listen to stories?

Once we have clarity on the purpose and practice of where we locate stories, we consider how we listen to stories. This is not a question of pragmatics, but rather one in which we explain our values and positionality in listening to stories. Storying is a multidirectional process of meaning making: of receiving and creating stories. Our practice of listening and receiving stories informs how we (re)create stories. We see both as very attuned emergent and responsive praxis.

## *Tracey*

One of the most supportive methodologies in Aboriginal storytelling, when shared in the confines of family and community, is that there will sometimes be more than one person who knows the story, who was present at the event/happening that is the source of the story and, as witness, is able to relay the story from their perspectives. On these occasions the storyteller, the one who is speaking, may be offered correctives, small details and emphasis that have been missed in the telling to the listener(s); thus there is added depth. For those of us who engage in research, these moments have equivalence to data/evidence verification. To be able to hear the story with that added richness, coming from more than the one storyteller, has further effect for a methodology of hearing. The dynamism of simultaneous multiple tellings of a story in one sense imprints on the listener's ears the importance, the urgency, the relevancy of the story for hearing, remembering, thinking about and archiving the story. It is also a dynamism for actualising Aboriginal relationality. What is it that the *I* of the listener needs to hear as the part of the *we* in belonging to family and community, keeping in mind that I am using *community* in a broad interpretation? For example, an Aboriginal familial community of immediate kin and friends as kin, or perhaps a scholarly Aboriginal community. Also, keeping in mind that I am speaking of stories in relation to colonisation – the observed behaviours and actions of the coloniser and the subsequent analysis and responses by Aboriginal people to those colonising behaviours and actions. Within this contextualisation then, my positioning of the *I* of the *we* cannot be separated from a politics of identity that acknowledges that I am bringing to the surface a component of the contextualisation which often remains unspoken. That is, identifying as Aboriginal is political in this country. Listening, then, is a methodology for merging into the story and with the storyteller, affirming the *we* in the *I* and the *I* in the *we* in shared community, within country/space and across times – a positionality and movement that enables the individual *I* agentic push from within and for the *we* collective.

Articulating meaning of emergent/immersed listening is a challenging task. Again, I refer to Paul Collis (2016), who provides the following insight:

> Those old storytellers, the same people who white governments dismissed as "un-knowers", they had power. Appearing at times to the

white world as "no-bodys", they were intelligent, gentle and responsible people. They looked "outward" upon the world and made comment
of the world in their art, leaving indelible marks upon my memory. In
their voice, they brought to life the imagined and the "un-imagined",
making them believable to me and to the others who listened. Those old
people taught and entertained.

Stories cannot be unheard and nor should they, for underneath lies a subtle
message, a learning for our lives.

### *Louise*

To hear the stories, I mean to really hear the stories, I listen intently to
those whose perspectives I seek, to see what emerges. I am inspired and
aligned with what Bronwyn Davies (2014) refers to as *emergent listening*, an
approach that draws from Henry Bergson's (1911) theory of creative evolution and Barad's (2007) theory of agential realism and diffractive analysis.
It involves noticing what emerges from what becomes automated, such as
our taken-for-granted practices and assumptions, which Bergson refers to
as *lines of descent* that "might be accomplished almost instantaneously, like
releasing a spring" (Bergson, 1911/2007, p. 7). So it is about noticing the
slip into the automated and refraining from an assumption and sitting and
being fully present to sense what really matters here. Sitting with questions,
sitting with discomfort, sitting with the unsettling. An inner work of ripening
or creating is welcomed, what Bergson refers to as *lines of ascent*. As Bronwyn Davies (2014) explains in her application of Bergson's thinking, lines
of descent and ascent continually affect and depend on each other. Though
"lines of descent may foreclose the emergence of new thought," through
recognition of such "they also create a coherent space in which the new can
emerge," space for lines of ascent which "are life-giving and powerful, but
they are not always good and may sometimes be sad and even dangerous"
(Davies, p. 8). With consideration of Bergson's ideas and Davies application,
I seek to let go of prior assumptions and categories and strive to be fully present to notice what emerges as mattering to those who tell me their stories.

I am also listening to my own internal dialogue, noticing thoughts as
they pass in and out – letting go of desire to fixate – noticing how ideas,
stories and observations affect each other. And when I research with young
children, much of their stories are heard by reading their bodies in action
with environments. I see and feel their stories played out before and in and
around me.

I share what I hear with what others hear around me, who were there in
the story moment too. Further perspectives flesh out what is heard. The

intent is not to story accurate accounts of events (though I admit I do often spend time searching contextual factors to support accuracy) but rather to story deeper understanding. To honour the principle that storying gives voice to the silenced margins, I share my storying back with those who I have listened to, to check whether it is the story they wanted to be heard.

## How do you bring stories to life?

This is a question of creativity. "How do you bring stories to life?" is also a question of "How do you (re)create a living story?" It is about our creative practice in storying: a poetic endeavour – a poiesis (making) with aesthesis (sensation that produces affect). We are creating to bring stories to life, so that the stories are felt as the lived experiences of the audience. We describe how we create to address and meet specific audiences. Our framing of "Which way?" has lead us to ponder "What are our responsibilities in and to story making?" "What medium do we use to bring stories to life?" "Have we done the stories right?" "Is the flesh fleshy on the bone of the medium?" and "Are we practised as story artisans?"

### *Tracey*

My first serious research effort in storying was in my doctoral studies. When I reflect on this time I acknowledge and appreciate the extent to which one has to be immersed, moving from text to text to draw out the theories and concepts that would best work with the research. And during this process you have to be focussed, keeping yourself apart, away from distractions. I came to live in my head, in this isolated, nerdy cocoon with the thoughts and words of theorists – white theorists, black theorists, women of colour theorists, and Indigenous theorising. I found "aha" moments in the work of theorists who wrote to decolonisation, antiracist strategy, the unpacking of white race privileges and so on, and I found style in those who wrote poetically, lyrically with and through theory. In taking myself into the text, the ways in which I was reading and understanding the messages, the word crafting, was something that I recognised, something I knew deep within my body. I was familiar with this skill. The familiarity came in the stories that my old people had told me. Another "aha" moment slapped me up the side of the head. The old people's telling of stories were theoretical texts too, and I wanted to give them equal value in my research. This is a long-winded response to how I bring stories to life, but an important first step is to make the stories known with all their vibrancy and verve.

The benefit I had is that I knew the stories by heart; they were told to me again and again and again. But what I had to do was to give the stories another skin, to find the way in which the story would survive the transfer from oral to written, from the private to the public, from Aboriginal audiences to highly likely white readers, without losing its essence. So I wrote creatively, imagining myself of the time and the moments, with the characters and the events. I placed myself in the story to imagine/observe what could and should be seen. In the written telling of the story, I wanted to draw the reader, sensually and carefully, into lives that are generally not known. My word crafting had to mirror the oral performances of those old people – the talking hands, face shapes and body nuances. The crafting was not easy. Through words I wanted to show the gasp of a breath in the horror of a story, in the drop of a tear the sadness of a story, in the slow nodding of a head, lips pursed upwards a thoughtfulness for the story, and the eyes wide crinkling of a forehead "I hadn't thought of that before" in a story. The crafting is not easy. It takes time – carefulness for holding something tender, a coaxing of the words to bring the light and make anew.

### *Louise*

I bring stories to life through embodied, emplaced storytelling. To me stories are most alive when performed. I struggle with the two-dimensionality of written stories. In the flesh, I can bring stories to life by changing the tone, pitch, volume and pace of my voice at carefully selected moments to create mood, emotion and affect. By embodying the story, I am there in the story and seek to making it the experience of those who are listening to the tale (Benjamin, 1968/1999, p. 87). In embodying the story, I am "an actor, an agent, a translator, an animator, and . . . a thief who robs treasures to give something substantive to the poor" (Zipes, 2005, p. 17). Zipes defines the collective pool of stories of humanity as treasures. As a storyteller, I collect stories that appeal, then transform them with my personal and ideological viewpoints to verbally and kinaesthetically bring these treasures to life before a chosen audience.

 I bring stories to life by sharing something of myself, by looking into the eyes of the audience to see what makes their eyes sparkle. Looking into the eyes of each other creates intimacy, drawing the listener in, as she identifies her life with those in the story. There are points of connection that resonate with listeners, for they may have had similar experiences or they can imagine that the same could happen to them. This intimacy can invoke a web of human relationships (Arendt, 1958/1998), as the connection between storyteller, story and listener cultivates connections with each other.

The relationship with others is at the core of bringing stories to life. It is about "inter-being" (Kristeva, 2001, p. 15) – the life of a story depends on being with others.

When storying in written form, the intimacy is cultivated through unashamedly using *I*, for they are the stories on which I have greatest authority – the ones I have lived – the ones in which I am embodied and emplaced within. I seek to bring the stories to life, through my voice interchanging with others, through tantalising sensorial descriptions, in the hope that the readers imagine they are there with me.

## How are stories gifted?

Once stories are brought to life, here we consider our practices of gifting stories. We name the practice of dedicated sharing as *gifting* to honour age-old tradition, the intimacy and bonding that deliberately shared storying nurtures. We don't just throw stories out into the ether. Our ethic is transgenerational movements for storying. We see stories as treasures and storying as reciprocal. The gifting is honoured with due protocol and responsibility, and crafted to specific audiences.

### *Tracey*

There are many gifts in storying. At an aesthetic level, whether through telling and performing, or through writing stories, there is entertainment – the sheer enjoyment of taking in a story that has not been heard before to learn something new or for affirming knowledge. The gift of being able to share stories creates bonds between the teller and the listener/reader. My intentions in gifting will vary with the audience. In Aboriginal social circles, storytelling is a shared responsibility. Having said that, not all people are storytellers, and different people will have different stories. The stories I have shared in this book are hopefully seen as gifts to members of my own family for remembering our old people and the lives which they were forced to live, allowing the descendants to learn from those times – to have new and hopefully uplifting stories. For other members of the Aboriginal community, my stories will have resonance, connecting through commonality of experiences, affirming our identities and strengthening our positionalities in a world that is not always safe nor sensitive. For the students of research, I share my work so that you have confidence to take on this approach of storying research as a legitimate form of knowledge production. There may be gifts also for those who are othered in the stories, offered to take strength from our differences. And for white academic readers, particularly those who struggle to have meaningful relationships with Aboriginal peoples and their place in this country as stolen lands. The meta-story about Aboriginal people needs to change. Have courage. Tell a different story. In Aboriginal principles of reciprocity, gifting has its responsibilities – to gift back.

*Louise*

There is a certain selflessness with storying. As the consistent thought when storying is of others – the careful guardianship of others' stories and the carefully packaging of these stories to gift to other readers/listeners/viewers. Storying comes with tremendous responsibility, because through storying you seek to nourish thought, body and soul; claim voice in the silent margins; invite embodied relational meaning making; intersect the past and present as living oral archives; and honour collective ownership and authorship. Storying gift giving is actually the most thoughtful gift I can imagine. Those stories that speak to you stay with you throughout your life, offering pearls of guiding wisdom at much-needed opportune moments. For example, I think of the Thai folk tale "The Freedom Bird" (Hartley, 1996) that I first heard Jewish storyteller Donna Jacobs Sife share. At the close of the story, she dedicated the story to people of Tibet and their fight for freedom. This stayed with me. It made me think about freedom, and the "sense and hold the fire in your belly" enduring fight for freedom. The story tells of how a hunter does every violent act he can think of to silence a bird because he does not like the bird's song: "naa-naa-na-na-naa – blrrrrrrrr" – a story we have seen played out throughout human history through genocide and ethnic cleansing. In time, the bird gathers with others and sings its song hundredfold. The surprising magnitude of numbers triggers a realisation by the hunter that you cannot "kill freedom".

The simplicity of the story makes it accessible to young children, and at first the gift they take is the joy of the bird's song – as they join in and laugh and continue to sing the bird's song all day. And then, say a year older, they start to ask questions like "Why does the hunter kill animals?" and "Who protects the animals from the hunters?" and make declarations of "We have to help save the animals" and "The freedom bird was trying to say something" (Phillips, 2010, pp. 112–113). Questions and understandings of freedom injustices start to emerge. And a few years later, tweens start to correlate the symbolism in the story with contemporary freedom struggles they are familiar with, such as asylum seekers in offshore detention centres. The story keeps giving. And for me personally, I have carried this story with me for nearly 20 years, gifting to children, teachers and student-teachers, provoking conversations on silencing, on language, on freedom struggles, on the power of collective voice. It was the first story I told in my practice of social justice storytelling, that I studied in my PhD. It began the conversation of injustices with 5-year-olds, to hear how they may seek to redress injustices through active citizenship. So many stories, inquiries, presentations, publications and achievements have been launched by that one story. Most recently I have been filmed telling that story, gifting it to children in detention in Nauru with hope for their freedom.

My research through, with and as storying is gifted performatively in presentations, so the audience is taken into the experience, into the wonderings, into the troublings. With published, written storying, I seek to gift it to those whose stories are there, and to those who I sense would appreciate, and to those who may learn from the storying.

## Together/two-gather

In this chapter, we two have gathered our thoughts to dialogue our approach to storying research. Our conversation commences with the important matter of ethical approaches to research with Aboriginal communities and with children. Our key message: do no harm. Through developing substantive relationships with Aboriginal Elders, professional staff, community members and children, for guidance and navigation, this objective can be attained. In discussing the source of storying, we find the source in our professional connections and the relational embodiments we are able to develop. The stories shared in Chapter 2 reveal the importance of our families' herstories as a source of storying, piecing together fragments through research to make whole, make richer. We detail how we use our tools of listening and enlivening stories, our techniques to story in research imagining, embodying, performing and writing. Finally, we lead our dialogue to storying as gift – our knowings of what it means to receive, to share, to pass on, to give back. Next, we share the diverse ways those in our communities story. In the final chapter, we revisit the key issues we have raised, speaking again of the principles, and end with an invitation for those who read this book.

## References

Anzaldua, G. (1990). *Making face, making soul/Haciendo caras: Creative and critical perspectives by feminists of color*. San Francisco, CA: Aunt Lute Books.

Arendt, H. (1998). *The human condition* (2nd ed.). Chicago: The University of Chicago Press (Original work published 1958).

Barad, K. (2007). *Meeting the universe halfway: Quantum physics and the entanglement of matter and meaning*. Durham: Duke University Press.

Benjamin, W. (1999). *Illuminations* (H. Zorn, Trans.). London: Pimlico (Original English version published 1968).

Bergson, H. (2007). *Creative evolution* (A. Mitchell, Trans.). London: MacMillan (Original work published in 1911).

Bunda, T. (2014). *The relationship between Indigenous peoples and the university: Solid or what!* (Doctoral thesis). University of South Australia, Australia.

Cannella, G. S., & Viruru, R. (2004). *Childhood and postcolonization: Power, education and contemporary practice*. New York: Routledge Falmer.

Collis, P. (2016). Remembers artists. *Westerly, 61*(1), 244–246.

Davies, B. (2014). *Listening to children: Being and becoming*. Abingdon, Oxon: Routledge.

Dudgeon, P., Kelly, K., & Walker, R. (2010). Closing the gaps in and through Indigenous health research: Guidelines, processes and practices. *Australian Aboriginal Studies*, *2*, 81–91.

Fredericks, B. (2007). Utilising the concept of pathway as a framework for indigenous research. *The Australian Journal of Indigenous Education*, *36*(1), 15–22.

Hartley, B. (1996). The freedom bird. In N. Livo (Ed.), *Joining in: An anthology of audience participation stories and how to tell them* (pp. 19–22). Cambridge, MA: Yellow Moon Press.

Kristeva, J. (2001). *Hannah Arendt: Life is a narrative* (R. Guberman, Trans.). New York: Columbia University Press.

Martin, K. (2010). Indigenous research. In G. Mac Naughton, S. A. Rolfe, & I. S. Blatchford (Eds.), *Doing early childhood research: International perspectives in theory and practice* (pp. 85–100). Maidenhead, UK: Open University Press.

Martin, K., & Mirraboopa, B. (2003). Ways of knowing, ways of being and ways of doing: A theoretical framework and methods for indigenous re-search and Indigenist research. *Journal of Australian Studies*, *76*, 203–221.

Nakata, N. (2007). The cultural interface. *The Australian Journal of Indigenous Education*, *36*, 7–14.

Phillips, L. G. (2010). *Young children's active citizenship: Storytelling, stories and social actions* (Doctoral thesis). Queensland University of Technology, Australia.

Rigney, D. (2010, December).The fourth stage of the centre's development, an overview: Ideas about future developments in Yunggorendi's research portfolio. Paper presented at *Yunggorendi Yarnin 2011–16*, Flinders University.

Smith, L. T. (2012). *Decolonising methodologies: Research and indigenous peoples* (2nd ed.). London: Zed Books.

Solorzano, D. G., & Yosso, T. J. (2001). Critical race and LatCrit theory and method: Counter-storytelling. *Qualitative Studies in Education*, *14*(4), 471–495.

Vivian, A., Jorgensen, M., Bell, D., Rigney, D. M., Cornell, S., & Hemming, S. J. (2016). Implementing a project within an indigenous research paradigm: The example of nation building research. *Ngiya: Talk the Law*, *5*, 47–69.

Zipes, J. (2005). To eat or be eaten: The survival of traditional storytelling. *Storytelling, Self, Society*, *2*(1), 1–20.

# 5   Sharing through storying

This chapter is designed as a sharing space. In the spirit of collectivity, we have brought together examples of storying from the communities we are connected to in Australia. The idea is to provide readers with a diverse range of examples to see and feel how some others share storied research, and to showcase the great storying work happening in Australia. It is through these examples we hope readers new to the idea of storying begin to imagine the possibilities. Examples were selected to provide a good cross-section of modes (visual, music, dance, drama, film, oral and written storytelling) and platforms (academic and public, published and live). In a way, what follows is an annotated bibliography, with a brief description of each work to guide you in your choice of works to locate and read (or view to see), and understand further what storying can be. The examples of research through storying are organised into two main sections: *performed, visual and embodied storying* (e.g., storied sculptures, film, dance, verbatim theatre, walks) and *written storying* (e.g., storied written works). Each section provides storying that has been shared across diverse platforms, from the conventional academic platforms (e.g., theses, conferences, academic journals and books), to a diverse range of public platforms (websites, public performances, films and walks). For each section, examples are listed alphabetically, with Aboriginal Australian examples that Tracey has carefully selected from her networks, and non-Indigenous examples that Louise has selected from her networks. In honouring the influence of place and heritage in storying, we acknowledge the heritage of each storying author. Our selections are largely informed by innovation and draw from emerging scholars (to seize an opportunity to showcase the innovation of their new work).

## Performed, visual and embodied storying

We have grouped here examples of storying research that have been performed, are visual or offer some embodied interaction with storying. We are foregrounding diverse modes of storying to purposefully disrupt the

DOI: 10.4324/9781315109190-5

privileging of the written word in academia. The works include storying through visual art, film, dance, verbatim theatre, sculpture and performative walks, music and photography. However, there is an inherent problem here in translating such three-dimensional work into two-dimensional words on pages. For some, we have been able to provide images and URLs to video footage and websites to enhance insight of what the performed, visual or embodied storying looked and felt like. For many of these storying examples, however, you really had to be there for the embodied emplaced experience of meaning making. As Joanne Archibald (2008) noted, whenever Indigenous oral tradition is presented in textual form, the text limits the level of understanding because it cannot portray the storyteller's gestures, tone, rhythm and personality (p. 17). And as Louise noted in her PhD thesis,

> Storytelling is a live experience. In this thesis I have included transcripts of the stories that I shared, but this is only part of the story. Like the accompanying video footage and audio recordings, they cannot capture the whole experience. Storytelling is an aesthetic encounter, so it was the sensory and affective expression between teller and audience that were difficult to capture. It is only through live experiences of storytelling that the nuances between teller and listener can be seen, heard, and felt all at the same time. For these reasons I am acutely aware that readers experience only part of the stories through transcripts.
>
> (p. 12)

These frustrations over the limitations of the written word on the page in a linear book have been felt throughout the development of this book. We hope that the words and images chosen provoke imaginings of lived embodied experiences. All of the examples in this section are by artist-researchers or arts-based researchers, and so they show storying rather than tell or explain storying.

**Balla, P., & Delany, M. (Curators). (2017).** *Sovereignty.* **Australian Centre for Contemporary Art, Melbourne, Australia.** *Find out more at* **https://acca.melbourne/exhibition/sovereignty/**
Paola Balla is a Wemba Wemba and Gunditjmara woman of Italian and Chinese heritage. She is a practising artist who curated *Sovereignty* with ACCA Artistic Director Max Delany. The curation of the storied exhibition sought to compose culturally and linguistically diverse stories of self-determination, identity, sovereignty and resistance from both contemporary and historical works of First Nations peoples of South-East Australia. *Sovereignty* was a platform for Indigenous community expression, and was accompanied by an extensive programme of talks, forums, screenings, performances, workshops, education programmes and events.

**Black, A. L., Crimmins, G., & Henderson, L. (2017, June).** *Storied, slow, aesthetic, relational: A wabi-sabi approach to doing and writing "research".* **AARE Theory Workshop, Southern Cross University, Gold Coast.** *Find out more at* **www.aare.**

**edu.au/data/Secretariat/Theory_Workshops/Gold_Coast/Workshop_bried_
and_bio_notes_v_3.pdf**

Through the concept of *wabi-sabi*, the Japanese art practice of honouring imperfections (cracks/breaks) in crockery, this workshop storied the cracks and crevices and rot of lived lives in academia. Ali, Gail and Linda storied their lives as women in academia, then invited participants to story their academic lives through words scribed on ceramic dinner plates. In small groups, storied lives in academia were shared, framed by the words scribed on the plates. Plates were then fragmented with the smashing force of a hammer and gifted to others in the group to each piece together a composite storied plate. The cracks of the composite plates were honoured with *kintsugi*-like golden repair, ethics of care, slow scholarship and story.

*Figure 5.1 Wabi-sabi* storying.

Photograph taken by Ali Back; permission to reproduce granted.

*Figure 5.2 Wabi-sabi* storied plates.

Photograph taken by Ali Back; permission to reproduce granted.

**Bunda-Heath, N. (Choreographer). (2017, August).** *Blood quantum.* **Arts House, Melbourne.**

This work is an exquisite piece of embodied intergenerational storying, blending story that is voiced over the choreography. Ngioka, Ngugi/Wakka Wakka and Birapi woman, has choreographed a duet that tells her matrilineal grandmother's story as written by her mother, Tracey Bunda. The dance work is a story that references eugenics for ascribing Aboriginal peoples and cultures as fragments of fragments. It is a story often hidden, but its telling allows Aboriginal people to heal from the legacies of colonisation. Through *Blood Quantum*, Ngioka is honouring her grandmother, and educating those who do not know about the history of the Stolen Generations in Australia.

*Figure 5.3  Blood Quantum* dancers Josh Twee and Claire Rodrigues.
Photograph taken by Bryony Jackson; permission to reproduce granted.

*Figure 5.4  Blood Quantum* dancers Josh Twee and Claire Rodrigues.
Photograph taken by Bryony Jackson; permission to reproduce granted.

*Figure 5.5 Blood Quantum* dancers Josh Twee and Claire Rodrigues.
Photograph taken by Bryony Jackson; permission to reproduce granted.

**Barker, L. L. (Writer/Director). (2014).** *My grandmother's country* **[Motion picture]. NSW, Sydney, Australia: Metroscreen, in association with Earthstar Productions & Screen NSW.** *To watch, go to* **www.sbs.com.au/ondemand/video/ 549148227796/Desperate-Measures**
Through film, Lorina Barker, Wangkumara and Muruwari woman, tells her grandmother's story of being trucked off Tibooburra country to Brewarrina Mission in the 1930s, making self-sufficient people ration dependent. The storied film has been pieced together from audio and photo archives, woven in with footage of Lorina's extended family's recent retracing of the journey back to her grandmother's country, to bring her spirit home.

**Ration Shed Museum Initiative.** *The Cherbourg Memory.* **Find out more at http://cherbourgmemory.org**
The Cherbourg Memory is an online database of memory storying of the Cherbourg community, a community formed as a government settlement under the Aboriginal Protection Act in 1904. Community members and descendants actively participate by adding their stories, searching for others and connecting with Cherbourg people. On this site you will find stories of dormitory living, black diggers, enforced labour, culture and language, and education and prominent people. Aboriginal readers, as lovers of photographs and stories, will be lost for hours. The stories shared are difficult and sometimes sad stories, but they are essential stories of survival and hope. The website is a critical contribution to the power of Aboriginal memory for the nation.

**Coleman, K. S. (2017).** *An a/r/tist in wonderland: Exploring identity, creativity and digital portfolios as a/r/tographer* **(Doctoral thesis). University of Melbourne, Australia.** *Find out more at* **www.artographicexplorations.com and http://hdl.handle.net/11343/124239**

This thesis is an extraordinary artistically storied treat by white Australian feminist, artist, researcher and teacher Kate, who was born and raised in Eora nation, and now lives and works in Kulin nation. Informed by theorists in critical, social and visual cultures in art education, Kate stories – through visual art and written words – how learning in and through a personalised portfolio, as both process and product, affects creativity and identity as an artist. The research is a/r/tographic (from the standpoint of artist-researcher-teacher). It embodied in its storying the importance of understanding creativity and creative practice for students as art makers and responders to art, as makers, historians, theorists and critics. The thesis as a whole provides storying of practice-based pedagogies through embodied praxis, portfolio pedagogies, storied personalised curriculum and creative and aesthetic digital curation for self-discovery and creativity.

Cooper, J. (2015). *Co-creating with, and in, a southern landscape* (Doctoral thesis). Victoria University, Melbourne, Australia. *Find out more at* http://vuir. vu.edu.au/30165/

As an artist and musician, white Australian Jayson entwines "place" in his creative work and thinking through arts-based autoethnography and music-based research. Jayson stories his place sense-making of Kulin nation's seven seasons through photography and music. He draws embodied sensorial connections as an artist, researcher and educator in relation to the conceptual and physical local landscapes of the colonised city of Melbourne that he moves through. The thesis presents an intertextual artistic and written celebration of the Wurundjeri landscape (a southern landscape), whilst Jayson critically gazes at his whiteness in relation to land, people, climates, skies, waterways and animals as he co-creates with, and in, the south. Through complex polyphonic layering and re-presentation, this thesis seeks to find ethical and inclusive overlaps between Aboriginal and non-Aboriginal knowledge and perspectives through genuine engagement with Aboriginal knowledge and culture, whilst maintaining consciousness and criticality of his whiteness.

Crimmins, G. (2014). *An arts-informed narrative inquiry into the lived experience of women casual academics* (Doctoral thesis). University of the Sunshine Coast, Australia. *To watch these representations, visit the following links:*

> Scene 1: https://era.library.ualberta.ca/downloads/bm326m184m
> Scene 2: https://era.library.ualberta.ca/downloads/bmg74qm16h
> Scene 3: https://era.library.ualberta.ca/downloads/sf268796c
> Scene 4: https://era.library.ualberta.ca/downloads/bpr76f347p
> Scene 5: https://era.library.ualberta.ca/downloads/0z709019x
> Epilogue: https://era.library.ualberta.ca/downloads/bvq27zn47c

Welsh woman Gail (now living on Gubbi Gubbi country) explored the lived experience of women casual academics in Australia. Using storying, the emotionally and cognitively lived experiences of six women casual academics were re-presented through story drama of proto-verbatim theatre (in which the words and stories of the participants are theatricalised). This genre of performative storying makes explicit the constructedness of the re-presentation, and cognitively and emotionally engages an audience in the stories of others. Gail purposefully selected the storying form for its congruency with the fully embodied stories of the research participants and their doubly othered status as women and casual academics. In Gail's written thesis she explains story-gathering processes and principles. She argues a case for the more feminist analytical practice of restorying, and the specific nuances of restorying into verbatim drama. The videos illustrate performative storying not only through drama but also through filmic devices, through the use of lighting, focus, angle and positioning, to subtly reflect the isolation and exploitation of casual academia for women.

**Foley, G., & Hawkes, J. (2012).** *Foley.* **Ilbijerri Theatre Company, Melbourne.** *Find out more at* **http://ilbijerri.com.au/event/foley/**

Gumbainggir activist, historian and warrior scholar Gary Foley provocatively stories untold black Australian history. He stories the lives, organisations and events of the Australian Black Power movement of the late 1960s and early 1970s, from his own lived memories as a key activist in the movement, interwoven with personal and fellow activists' archives, media reports, academic accounts and recent publicly available ASIO (Australian Security Intelligence Organisation) files. Gary Foley's composite storying reveals profound insight into land rights, native title, treaty, reconciliation, referendum, tent embassy, black power and black pride. The performance recounts his politically contextualised life as a riveting tale of resistance and determination. This creative work was a performative publication of ideas and arguments developed during his PhD candidature.

**Heckenberg, R. (Creative director). (2016).** *Yindyamurra sculpture walk.* **Murray River, NSW.** *Find out more at* **www.alburycity.nsw.gov.au/leisure-and-culture/ walking-and-cycling-trails/yindyamarra-sculpture-walk**

Wiradjuri researcher and artist Robyn Heckenberg worked with a team of local Aboriginal artists to story the place that links Wonga Wetlands with the South Albury Trail. Local people's stories of their connections to the river were collectively told and shared, and local artists worked with these ideas and their own lived experiences to create sculptural works that story Wiradjuri Country. Each work tells its own stories, and collectively the sculpture walk tells a larger story of Wiradjuri law, of Wiradjuri ways of being and doing, of respecting country, of enacting UN Declaration of Rights of Indigenous Peoples and of Indigenous research methodologies.

**Nanni, G., & James, A. (Playwrights). (2010).** *Coranderrk: We will show the country.* **La Mama Court house Theatre, Melbourne.** *Find out more at* **www.minute sofevidence.com.au/performance/**

Italian and South African writer-historian Giordano Nanni (now living in Kulin nation) and Yorta Yorta playwright Andrea James – as members of the Minutes of Evidence project team – collaborated to story the 141-page minutes of evidence of the 1881 Parliamentary Coranderrk Inquiry into a verbatim-theatre performance script. The Coranderrk Inquiry was a rare occasion in 19th-century Victoria when there was an official commission that heard Aboriginal witnesses on their calls for land and self-determination. The performative storying of the inquiry was designed to expose broad audiences to this rare moment in Australian history, and to provoke public conversations on questions of structural justice and reconciliation within, and between, Indigenous and non-Indigenous communities. The play has had five seasons and multiple one-off performances, and an annotated version of the script has been published with Aboriginal Studies Press in 2013. The website documents the prolific range of outputs from this provocative storying that brought together law, history and social sciences researchers, educators and artists.

**Phillips, L. G., Owen, A., Borland-Sentinella, D., & Peirano, E. (2016, 7–8 May).** *Walk with me* **[Performative walk of walking research findings]. Anywhere Festival. Brisbane.** *Find out more at* **http://louptales.education/walk-with-me-anywhere-festival/**

A performative storied walk experience which explores how walking can cultivate ethico-politico-urban wonder through awareness and interactions with others and public spaces. The walk was designed to provoke experiential encounters that foregrounded key concepts gleaned from Louise's research of walking arts projects. Accompanied by a duo of improvisers (Alice Owen and Deanna Borland-Sentinella, European Australians) in role as mad research assistants, Dr LouP facilitated walking encounters to activate embodied sensorial, exploratory and political awareness of self and others in public spaces. Provocative clues of a missing person spotted along the walk storied the concept of indeterminacy, leading to a rare sighting of a mermaid (Elena Peirano, Uruguayan) on the banks of Brisbane River, and meeting the local councillor to reflect on storied learnings of ethico-politico-urban wonder.

*Figure 5.6* Dr LouP greets walk participants.

Photograph taken by Martin Ambrose; permission to reproduce granted.

*Figure 5.7* Orleigh Park Manifesto launch.

Photograph taken by Martin Ambrose; permission to reproduce granted.

*Figure 5.8* Mermaid on the bank of the Brisbane River.

Photograph taken by Martin Ambrose; permission to reproduce granted.

## Written storying

Here, we have gathered a selection of written forms of research through, with and as storying across largely traditional research-output forms of articles, theses, books and book chapters. This selection is from our communities in Australia. Many of the authors are colleagues or recommended by colleagues. Most of the examples are largely recent works that illustrate and explore storying concepts of collectivity, place, identity, embodiment and intersecting of the past and present. The authors are diverse across origins, and the storied topics explore a range of prevalent topics that include academia, archaeological records, belonging, connection to country, domestic violence, marginalisation, black-white race relations and sacred storytelling. We hope that amidst these examples of written storying, you see diverse possibilities of theorising and enacting storying.

Birch, A. (2002). *Framing Fitzroy: Contesting and (de)constructing place and identity in a Melbourne suburb* (Doctoral thesis). University of Melbourne, Australia. *and* Birch, A. (2015). *Ghost river.* Brisbane: University of Queensland Press. *Find out more at* https://thegarretpodcast.com/tony-birch/
Tony Birch is a well-known Aboriginal writer, activist and academic, and currently holds the position of professor at Victoria University. When Tony wrote his doctoral thesis at Melbourne University (2002), he theorised the negative social construction of the Melbourne suburb of Fitzroy. Tony continues his storying of living in the margins in his novel, *Ghost River*, which won the 2016 Victorian Premier's Literary Award for Indigenous Writing. His other award-winning works include *Blood*, which was shortlisted for the Miles Franklin Award. He is also the author of *Shadowboxing*, and two short-story collections, *Father's Day* and *The Promise*.

Black, A. L., Crimmins, G., & Jones, J. K. (2017). Reducing the drag: Creating V formations through slow scholarship and story. In S. Riddle, M. Harmes, & P. A. Danaher (Eds.), *Producing pleasure in the contemporary university* (pp. 137–156). Rotterdam, the Netherlands: Sense Publishing.
Ali (English-French heritage), Gail (Welsh heritage) and Janice (Scottish-Irish heritage) liken their practice of collective storying to how flying birds cooperatively work in energy-boosting V formations. Learning by watching the one in front, and sensing what is happening in the surrounds and responding accordingly, the authors note the conditions that support their writing flow. Locating pleasure, connectedness, interest and joy in their collective deliberate storying and re/de/storying of lived experiences, the authors resist the insidious, diminishing drag of managerialism, comparison and metric-based audits of productivity and outputs. They recognise the joy and pleasure of responding to longings to connect, to "care for self and others", and to "be" differently in academia through collective storying found in opportunities to listen and to converse in meaningful ways – ways that give time to reflection and relationship, ways that enable cooperative work and speaking lives into the academy.

Cutcher, A. J. (2015). *Displacement, identity and belonging: An arts-based, auto/biographical portrayal of ethnicity and experience.* Rotterdam, the Netherlands: Sense Publishers.
Story is a central motif of Lexi's arts-based auto/biographical inquiry of belonging and identity as a second-generation Hungarian-Australian. Lexi stories her and her family's cultural and displacement identities through family stories, memoirs, artworks, photographs and poetry. Through stories and self-created artworks, Lexi elicits provocative reflections and interrogations of ethnicity, migration, place, marginalisation, memory and self, drawing on historical, cultural and political perspectives. Lexi's storying and collage work evokes emplaced visceral intimacy of each family member's lived experience, like a living, breathing photo album. *Displacement, Identity and Belonging* is a beautiful example of storying as theory, as research, as art and as a good story.

Gilbey, K. (2014). *Privileging First Nations knowledge: Looking back to move-forward* (Doctoral thesis). Batchelor Institute of Indigenous Tertiary Education, Batchelor, Australia.
This thesis is a counter story to the dominant narrative of the Batchelor Institute being just another Aboriginal organisation that was run into the ground by Aboriginal incapacity. It was written to highlight the subtle hidden ways that racist ideologies infiltrate an Indigenous tertiary-education workplace. Alyawarre woman Kathryn has, through storying, highlighted critical moments of daily interactions and encroachments on the operations of the institute to highlight the small, myriad and complex ways that racist ideologies are enacted. It illustrates how mimicry, interdiction, subjection and abjection are all tools that serve to maintain ignorance, which in turn serves to maintain white privilege. Kathryn argues that by trusting in old Aboriginal cultures that have never really disappointed, Aboriginal people can regain pride and belief in this organisation as a transformed First Nations site of scholarship, learning and cultural celebration.

Hardy, D. (2015). *BOLD: Stories from older lesbian, gay, bisexual, transgender and intersex people.* The Rag & Bone Man Press Inc, Panton Hill, Victoria. *Find out more at: www.youtube.com/watch?v=UIFxd5QrtGU*
David Hardy is an Indigenous doctoral graduate of the Batchelor Institute (2015). His book shines a spotlight on the stories of more than 50 older members of the LGBTI community. The stories tell of first love, family, struggles and pride from ordinary and extraordinary people from diverse origins. As such, it is an important contribution to written storying and brings together a diverse group of people, often on the silenced margins, to tell their stories.

Henderson, L. G., Honan, E., & Loch, S. (2016). The production of the academicwritingmachine. *Reconceptualizing Educational Research Methodology, 7*(2), 4–18.
Three white Australian women – Linda (living on Boonwurrung/Bunurong country), Eileen (living on Jagera/Turrbal country) and Sarah (living on Gadigal country) – story the experience of the push to "publish or perish" in academic writing. They story how they experiment with merging as LindaEileenSarah – an

academicwritingmachine. Using digital platforms, such as Instagram, story-sharing conversations emerge from LindaEileenSarah with a differing rhythm created from chaos, from resistance to the hyperindividualized neoliberal university. LindaEileenSarah interrogate the machinic arrangements of the academicwritingmachine, through collaborative, metaphoric and poetic writing of lived stories of negotiating the counting of academic writing. The construction and constriction of the lived experiences of presenting, rewriting, reviewing, rejecting and resubmitting is restoried to craft imaginative, creative and joyous collective experiences.

**Josephs, C. (2008). The way of the s/word: Storytelling as emergent liminal. *International Journal of Qualitative Studies in Education, 21*(3), 251–267.**
White Australian artist, storyteller, educator and researcher Caroline stories her journey of becoming a storyteller, through personal reflections, drawings and dreams, other writers and theorists, interwoven with the telling of a Japanese Zen story "The Teaching". It is a story about facing death. The symbolism embedded in "The Teaching" illustrates principles of emerging methodologies and Caroline's storytelling learnings and being in the liminal – a transitionary phase of life. "The Teaching", like the other sacred stories Caroline worked with in her thesis, dealt with the liminal space between that which is unknowable or inconceivable, to understand the "sacred". Caroline draws on all the senses to bring to life the storying processes of weaving together memory, thought and what emerges and what departs in each moment for the storyteller and story listeners, as a story is enacted and embodied.

**Metta, M. (2015). Embodying Mêtis: The braiding of cunning and bodily intelligence in feminist storymaking. *Outskirts Online Journal, 32.* Retrieved from www.outskirts.arts.uwa.edu.au/volumes/volume-32/marilyn-metta**
Chinese-Malaysian-born Australian woman Marilyn Metta draws from the storied wisdom of Greek goddess Metis (as the concept of embodied intelligence) to poetically story her lived experiences of domestic abuse. Marilyn stories to reclaim Metis/*mêtis* for its metamorphic power. She reads and engages with power as somatically and materially experienced by bodies in ways in which language struggles to define and describe. Metis/*mêtis* is traced in her own poetic feminist story making and knowledge making of domestic violence, analysed through the symbolism of Greek mythology and Elizabeth Grosz's notions of becomings and freedom. Her poetic storying enacts embodied intelligence (*mêtis*): "Mêtis resides in our breath-work, our shadow-work, she slithers in between words and forms the slippery shadows of breath."

**Moreton, R. (2006). *The right to dream* (Doctoral thesis). University of Western Sydney, Australia. Retrieved from http://uwsprod.uws.dgicloud.com/islandora/object/uws%3A2495/datastream**
Dr Romaine Moreton is from the Goenpul Jagara people of Stradbroke Island and the Bundjulung people of northern New South Wales. Her thesis, *The Right to Dream*, proposes an Indigenous philosophy of storytelling and embodied knowledge. It explores the impact of the English language upon the Indigenous body affected through colonisation, offering an analysis of Aboriginality as a social and political construct resulting in the imposition of an inauthentic subjective

experience on sovereign Indigenous peoples, investigating its temporal and bio-logical consequence. *The Right to Dream* also explores the temporality of Indig-enous ancient cosmologies, the intelligence inherent in Indigenous chosen modes of communication and the ways in which Indigenous peoples "write" and "read" the earth-space. It is, in other words, the treatment of Indigenous cosmological, philosophical and religious practices as an expression of an Indigenous literature. *The Right to Dream* also explores the development of western textual culture, lin-earity and the invention of historicity as a way of controlling language, bodies and land by restricting individual access to discourse. Other storying works by Dr Romaine Moreton include a large-scale transmedia storytelling exhibition, *One Billion Beats*, in collaboration with the Campbelltown Arts Centre (see https:// vimeo.com/121083217).

**Wilson, C. J. (2017).** *Holocene archaeology and Ngarrindjeri Ruwe/Ruwar (land, body, spirit): A critical Indigenous approach to understanding the Lower Mur-ray River, South Australia* **(PhD dissertation, archaeology). Flinders University, Adelaide, Australia.**
Ngarrindjeri archaeologist Christopher Wilson stories a "Ngarrindjeri archaeologi-cal standpoint", through exploration of the researcher's lived experiences and prior knowledge and relationship to the Ngarrindjeri community, with critique of colonial practices (archives, representations and scientific investigations). Through intersec-tion of these multiple sources (in both written and visual form), he posits more holistic interpretations of archaeological records. Christopher's identity and lived experiences as a Ngarrindjeri man enable Ngarrindjeri epistemologies, critical the-ory, standpoint theory and Indigenous archaeologies to be foregrounded.

**Wooltorton, S., Collard, L., & Horwitz, P. (2015). Stories want to be told: Elaap Karlaboodjar.** *PAN: Philosophy, Activism, Nature, 11,* **3–18.**
This article is an important Western Australian contribution to written storying research. It investigates the many stories surrounding Elaap, the Leschenault Estua-rine System. *Elaap* is a Noongar word which means "on or by the water", refer-ring to the people and their place. *Nitja Noongar boodjar, derbal* – this is Noongar country and estuary. The authors purpose stories for defining relationality through identity and positionality through place. Additionally, the authors consider stories as lived, coauthored, embodied with land, and as tools for meaning making. They see stories as discursively formed in the human/spirit project. The authors evoke the story of Elaap for re-energising the land and its people.

## Together/two-gather

We hope that in this selection of research through, with and as storying, you see diverse ways and possibilities for storying. We searched across disci-plines we engage with and deliberated for considerable time over selections in order to provide diversity in modes and platforms, so that they also inspire further innovations in storying work. The parameters of what is and isn't storying were constantly debated. The process was actually quite unsettling and in many ways messed with central ideas of storying being fluid and inclusive. So in no way is this list definitive. And many of the authors may not name and claim their work as storying, but from our opening definition of storying as the act of making and remaking meaning through stories, we see that their work is illustrative of such.

In the final chapter, we revisit the principles of storying to propose ways to continue enactment of these principles in research, and invite readers to add to the ideas raised in this book.

# References

Archibald, J. (2008). *Indigenous storywork: Educating the heart, mind, body, and spirit*. Vancouver: UBC Press.

Phillips, L. G. (2010). *Young children's active citizenship: Storytelling, stories and social actions* (Doctoral thesis). Queensland University of Technology, Australia.

# 6 Ongoing advocacy for storying

We don't see ourselves as experts in storying. Rather, we have sought to create this book to carve a more recognisable space for storying in academia, and to have more focused conversations on what storying is, and can be, across diverse communities. We have argued that storying, as the act of making and remaking meaning through stories, is what researchers can, and do, in the propositions/conceptualisations of research, in the gathering of data with others, in the theorising and analysis of data and in the presentation and sharing of research. Storying is an ethically value-driven way of being and knowing the world through story. The central concept to foreground the word and form *story* is driven by motivations of inclusivity – to welcome and broaden audiences.

We see storying offering imaginative agency that has resonance with Appadurai's (2004) arguments that acts of (re)imagining future worlds are important social and material processes that create new "ethical horizon[s] within which more concrete capabilities can be given meaning, substance and sustainability" (p. 82). As such, they move us "away from wishful thinking to thoughtful wishing" (p. 82). For Indigenous peoples to exercise such agency of thoughtful wishing within, and speaking to social spaces that are inhabited – but which also displace us to the margins – offers substantive possibilities to expand ethical horizons, pushing against those spaces to grow larger in both vision and practice.

In our closing words on research through, with and as storying, we revisit the five *principles of storying* that were discussed in Chapter 3, to consider ways on how to move forward through these principles – ways to advocate further for the claiming of territory for storying. What we suggest are beginning threads that we hope readers continue to add to by messaging us through our Storying Research Facebook page at www.facebook.com/storyingresearch/.

DOI: 10.4324/9781315109190-6

## Advocating for nourishing thought, body and soul through storying

> The people were one with the stories and the stories one with the people, and every tale both embodied and sustained the whole.
>
> (Kwaymullina, 2014)

Such soothing words from Aboriginal academic, writer and illustrator Amberlin Kwaymullina, touching on the ontological essence of Aboriginal being – the first storytellers of this country. And it is in country that thought, body and spirit are nourished. Storying our differences as Aboriginal and white are well evident, but we do well to remember that in story there are connections, moments when our shared humanity is mobilised, crossing the divide of contestations and confrontations, moments that give us permission to breathe and know that in stories there are many faithful followers. Stories represent possibility for unity in our varied positions and a deep respecting of the need to be separate, knowing that the project of pulverising sameness drains our essence. Stories are sustenance and we all gladly partake.

Stories are warming, amusing, bemusing, intriguing, heavy-hearted and so good to tell and hear. They invite us to take a moment out of constant doing, to listen and feel another's life – to remind us we are embodied, relational beings. When Louise was first awarded the title Dr, she celebrated by putting a sign on her office door that read, "stories prescribed for most every condition". Though the sign was offered in jest, we see that stories bring wisdom to situations, and Louise did wish she had a story to offer every condition. As an antithesis to the meritocratic agenda of contemporary universities always on the hunt for measuring impact, feminist circles are starting to advocate for the creation and assertion of feminist metrics that show acts of kindness and care (personal communication, K. Allen, August 9, 2017). Perhaps the gifting of a story could be one of those acts of kindness and care – a cup of tea and a story to ease your ails. The power of the influence of stories should never be underestimated.

There is a growing trend, especially amidst feminist academics (such as Henderson, Honan, & Loch, 2016; Black, Crimmins, & Jones, 2017, noted in Chapter 5), of seeking to story about the lived experience of academia collectively, to give space to weeping wounds, to air seething rage and in the collectivity to be nourished through relationality and the comfort of "I'm with you, sister." Academics aren't just storying about what they research, but also about the experience of being an academic. Such storying is carving and claiming moments of pleasure. Books such as *Producing Pleasure in the Contemporary University* (Riddle, Harmes, & Danaher, 2017) provide an avenue for pleasurable storying in the academy. Pleasurable (as in relaxed and relatively unrestrained) storying is also effervescent through academic blogging.

The agency of self-managed public platforms for dissemination, like blogs, shake loose the shackles of restraint that academic writing imposes.

And so we encourage you to seek out stories and storying opportunities to warm off the chilling effects of the neoliberal university (and society at large), to provide nourishment and sustenance for the endurance of the incessant demands that never stop and creep into every crevice of every waking hour. More and more storying is entering conference presentations, and as arts-based research gains more momentum, more diverse, innovative and creative ways of storying research are emerging. Seek and create nourishment for your whole of being through storied walks, films, websites, drama, dance, songs, books and adventures.

## Advocating for the silenced margins through storying

In Chapter 3 and in writing of this principle, Tracey offered the story of the taking of her mother and her siblings – young lives sutured into the disciplining effect of colonisation. This story, brought forth from a historical margin into the present, has purposefully taken the oral form into the written so that Tracey's old people's voices could be heard beyond the safe confines of family guppatea conversations. In the telling of our stories, in the speaking of the words, decolonisation commences. In this country, in Australia, deep understanding of Aboriginal people's lives still remains easily negated with a loaded dismissive, an "If only they were the same as us," alluding to intolerance. Aboriginal stories from the margin bear witness to a more complete story of the nation, where its fullness offers the possibility of educative effect, and where a willingness to learn from Aboriginal others is a talking walk to epistemological change. Giving voice to our stories creates a healing, a knowing that our voices weave back into age-old traditions, enabling our bodies to thread seamlessly with the veracity of our spiritual selves.

The photograph shows my surgical scar after a heart attack. Oh my, my heart was nearly silenced forever. I am wrapped in a woollen scarf knitted by a member of my family, given to me by another member of my family. I am wrapped in warm love and care. I had asked Paola to take the photograph not knowing that she was not well herself. From that moment of deep vulnerabilities we have grown in strength – new stories have emerged, stitched into our lives. My heart beats on.

Worby, with Anangu scholar Tur and Rosas Blanch (of Yidniji/Ybarbarm peoples) (2014) writes of the preciousness of Aboriginal/black storying from the margins:

> Telling Black stories is important for historical, cultural, political and personal reasons. Each act of creation or re-creation adds to a store of precious resources which contributes to well-being, healing and the

*Figure 6.1* Embodied storying.

Photograph taken by Paola Balla; permission to reproduce granted.

capacity to imagine change. Stories sustain communities. Some writers come from lines of story keepers, song makers and Elders on country. With the authority of continuity, they write us forward. Other writers lack that direct, guiding narrative authority and – beginning with only fragments – write their way back to wholeness. At some point these writing pathways meet to reshape or restore ideas of time, space and country. They thread through all kinds of private and public, real and imagined spaces – sea country, desert country, parks, lounge rooms, sports grounds, libraries, classrooms – and those who travel with their stories are not always writers in one medium. They sing, dance, paint, and talk them as well. Each expression finds a new shape for dynamic language and – sometimes – ways of sharing that language with writers from other traditions.

(p. 1)

Tracey recalls that when we commenced this book, she boldly claimed that Aboriginal peoples talked in story all the time, noting it is the basis of conversations, fundamental to Aboriginal ways of being and knowing. There is a cacophony of Aboriginal voices at the margin – stories are all around, in dance, in art, in performance and in writing. The extent to which Aboriginal people story research to each other is self-evident. Common histories, embodiments of shared experiences, inform collective senses of what it means to be Aboriginal. There is a honey-lined richness in those voices. The value of Aboriginal stories for those who are outside our circles of storying – at the white centre – will be found in whether or not Aboriginal stories can be heard. For white readers of this book, there are lessons in listening. Hone the aural senses, allow Aboriginal words to lay upon your ears, to seep in – morph into a new skin. For Aboriginal readers, and particularly those who do not see themselves as writers or theorists, take courage. Your words, your stories, are important. Dominance understands the power of the written word. We do not advocate a black versioning of storying to replicate dominance in a different colour. We advocate because in writing, in taking black thought, words and stories to the white page, there is liberation.

## Advocating for embodied relational meaning making through storying

In celebrating and claiming research through, with and as storying, we assert the foregrounding of bodies (of the somatic, of the corporeal) and relationality to provoke deep, whole-of-being understanding of phenomena that can speak to audiences across sectors of society. We especially assert the welcoming of more performative, visual and embodied research through storying across a breadth of modes, as provided in the illustrative examples in Chapter 5. Break away from the dominant dissemination pattern of academic articles and books. Relish the greater embodied meaning that imagery and live performative interactivity can offer through, say, a single-hand gesture or dancing eyes. Position and frame bodies as agential and active entities in storying that can resist the operations of ideologies and forces of power. And when traditional platforms (e.g., books and articles) are chosen, the place of bodily sensation and emotion is integral in the storied words.

We encourage proliferation of research through storied films, dances, theatrical pieces, exhibitions and walks, so that innovation and relationality of phenomena with broad audiences is celebrated and maximised. Arts-based research is forging the way in this space. In arts-based educational research (ABER), both the American Educational Research Association (AERA) (www.abersig.com) and the British Education Research Association (BERA) (www.bera.ac.uk/group/arts-based-educational-research)

have well-established, specifically focused arts-based educational research groups. Canadian artist-researcher-teacher Rita Irwin has recently initiated the Network of Arts-Based Educational Research (NABER; see www. facebook.com/NetworkABER/) as a space to share ABER publications, theses and events, avenues and institutions supportive of ABER. In the Australian review of excellence in research, arts-based research outputs are classified as "Non-Traditional Research Outputs" and are required to have accompanying research statements that indicate research questions, contribution and significance if nominated for ERA (excellence in research for Australia) peer review (http://www.arc.gov.au/sites/default/files/filedepot/Public/ERA/ERA%202018/ERA%202018%20Submission%20Guidelines.pdf). NABER also seeks to share how arts researchers have successfully used research statements to argue the significance of the creative work by mapping circles of influence. By being embodied and relational, we see great potential in storying communicating deep, resonant meaning to broad audiences – not just academia, but the general public – across ages, across classes, across cultures.

We also advocate for being fully present in being with storying others. Seek out others who embrace embodied storying, and be and soak up the vibrant energy of that whole-of-being meaning making. For about 10 years now, Louise has been meeting up with a group (mostly women known as Wunderfools; www.facebook.com/Wunderfools/) on a relatively weekly basis, in the central room of a community house, to share improvised stories through movement. The group takes turns to perform for each other, inviting others into their stories as they choose. Sometimes a soundtrack to the performance is chosen by the lead performer/storyer, defined through a single word (e.g., *still*). The embodied stories emerge. They are created in the moment, through performers responding to each other's offers. At the close of the performance, the performer and those who have watched the emergent storying then share what they liked about the performed storying. This is a delightfully nurturing space, in which the group completely submerges in embodied relational storying, in which members have laughed and cried so much that their bodies ache.

## Advocating for intersecting the past and present title as living oral archives through storying

In our research for this book it became abundantly clear that Aboriginal people story. Storying research is an emergent trend. In the academy, Aboriginal scholars and students' works will be situated with stories – writing vignettes to tell of country, the history of country and what happened to country; to have locatedness with family; to apply theories to data collections; to centre their thinking. Tracey's story of her father as a young boy offered in Chapter 3 represents these elements, and we remind the reader of the Aboriginal contributions to the scholarly works of storying in Chapter 5 of the book. Paola Bella, Wemba Wemba and Gunditjmara warrior woman, as cocurator of the exhibition *Sovereignty* (2017) brought forth stories in art of a critical issue at a critical time in our lives, when constitutional reform is a contemporary and contentious (in both black and white senses) topic on the nation's political table. Storying of sovereignty, self-determination and resistance are agentic acts of being Aboriginal, discursively formed from the point of first (black/white) contact, which has not dissipated with time. In the Victorian Museum, the *Sovereignty* exhibition (2017) had synergy with Warriors of Aboriginal Resistance, enacting sovereignty through protest in the heart of Melbourne on Flinders Street. Lorina Barker's film *My Grandmother's Country* (2014) is a remembering, a piecing together of the fragments of fragments of her grandmother's story – an oral archive to story her spirit into country. Lorina continues the trend of storying in the medium of film, following in the footsteps of other Aboriginal women filmmakers such as Muruwari woman Essie Coffey. The Cherbourg Memory speaks back into living memories to document stories across time and into the light, free from the dark spaces of silence and forgetting. As with other Aboriginal keeping places, the Cherbourg Memory is an important theoretical and physical artefact for remembering. Robyn Heckenberg's *Yindyamurra Sculpture Walk* (2016) is a facilitation of stunningly beautiful sculptural works through working with Aboriginal community, and has brought to life the storying of long-held and loving connections to country, framed within a rights discourse. Wiradjuri oral archives breathe into the sculptures, resuscitating stories of the past into the present. In her doctoral thesis, *Privileging First Nations Knowledge: Looking Back to Move Forward* (2014), Alyawarre warrior woman and scholar Kathryn Gilbey has storied research from the perspective of educational self-determination, in all its complexities, to form a new archive entry of resistance within Aboriginal community agentic being. Goenpul Jagara Bundjulung scholar Romaine Moreton uses her PhD thesis, *The Right to Dream* (2006), to offer the reader storying research through an Aboriginal philosophy to redream our being, dedicating her work to the ancestors before, after and in the subliminally named space of the everywhen. The Nigerian storyteller Ben Okri (1997) offers the following wisdom:

> In a fractured age, where cynicism is god, here is a possible heresy: we live by stories, we also live in them. One way or another we are living the stories planted in us early or along the way, or we also living the stories we planted – knowingly or unknowingly – in ourselves. We live

stories that either give our lives meaning or negate it with meaningless. If we change the stories we live by, quite possibly we change our lives.

(p. 46)

As Aboriginal peoples, the embodying of stories from the oral to the written, performed, painted and danced, are respectful acts of remembering the teachings of ancestors, living oral archives linking the past with the present. Aboriginal ancestors' agencies for survival should be honoured, particularly when conventions are disrupted and norms challenged. Storying research does this. It is a breaking of tradition, yet easily lends itself to the gifts of Aboriginal stories. We advocate for the creation of safe and sensitive spaces for this to be realised. In reference to the academy, Aboriginal engagements can be fraught. Tracey's colleague who engaged in her doctoral studies (2014) as a research participant and who Tracey named, in relational terms, as Deadly Tidda Far South and Far West of My Country, named "universities as frightening, dangerous places" (p. 102). If Aboriginal entry into the university is to have real meaning, then there needs to be real respect for the stories that Aboriginal people carry, stories that will knowingly bring change to the way in which knowledge is (re)produced.

## Advocating for collectively owned and authored stories and storying

Though the contemporary university is built on the neoliberal individual, collectivity nurtures belonging, strengthens voice and ethically honours all contributors. We ethically argue for honouring the collectivity of storying, and seeking and claiming ways to enjoy collective storying. And in these troubled times, as Harraway (2016) contends, we need to "stay with trouble", which requires "unexpected collaborations and combinations, in hot compost piles" (p. 4). So, we recommend being open to unexpected bedfellows in collaborative storying. "Hot compost piles" imply the bringing together of layers of organic matter, of biodegradable waste that heat up and decompose. Louise has a newly found ritual of taking her family compost to a local community garden every couple of days. It's about a 10-minute walk down a hill, trespassing through a school, across a field and over a creek, to then reveal a hidden playfield and community garden. When the communal compost bin is reached and the lid lifted, the heat and odour is immediately sensed. Sensory memories of other places and times are evoked. Louise tips her organic matter on top of her neighbours' heating, festering fruit and vegetable waste. A momentary noting of the array: egg shells, banana skins, eggplant . . . Over time the combined organic matter heats, ferments, biodegrades and merges. Then when the time is right, someone will dig it over and dig it into the communal vegetable, fruit and herb gardens to enrich growth. The metaphor of the communal hot compost pile offers rich understandings and provocations for advocating and enacting collective storying in contemporary times. It is not easy. It is not at our doorsteps (for convenience). We have to commit time and mobility in emplaced connection to neighbourhoods to get to the place of collectivity (and maybe it requires traversing private or prohibited spaces). So we have to look outwards and make time for, and move to be with, others. The matter that nurtures us is the same matter that nurtures the merging of collective contributions for collective storying. Like the decomposing process, collective storying takes time, heat, fermentation and sensation. Though the potential rich luscious growth makes it oh so worthwhile.

Slow scholarship (Mountz et al., 2015) provides the ideal conditions for collectively owned and authored storying, and "good scholarship requires time: time to think, write, read, research, analyze, edit and collaborate"

*Figure 6.2* Storied growth from hot compost piles.
Original Artwork by Louise.

(p. 1237). A commitment to work collectively and to claim due time is a political act in these neoliberal times. And combined with slowness is care: care for self, care for collaborators and care for the work to give it due time. The Women Who Write Collective (n.d.), who collectively story, care for each other by taking turns to lead the storied writing in a synergistic way, responding to each other's demands and needs through an ethic of care. The Res-Sisters too enact care through their collective storying, through the collective decision that their collective work can be counted by whichever member of the collective needs the publication to count to support job security and progression (personal communication, Kim Allen, August 9, 2017). To sustain the collective voice in neoliberalism, we encourage looking outwards, taking time to meander, to relate and sensate – making and honouring those rich, slow, pungent, hot composting piles.

## Together/two-gather: storying reflections and actions

We would really welcome your readers' responses to what we have offered in this book. This is a starting conversation that builds on the legacy of many previous conversations of those who have storied before us.

## References

Appadurai, A. (2004). The capacity to aspire: Culture and the terms of recognition. In R. Vijayendra & M. Walton (Eds.), *Culture and public action* (pp. 59–84). Stanford: Stanford Social Sciences.

Balla, P., & Delany, M. (Curators). (2017). *Sovereignty*. Australian Centre for Contemporary Art.

Barker, L. L. (Writer/Director). (2014). *My grandmother's country* [Motion Picture]. NSW, Australia: Metroscreen in association with Earthstar Productions & Screen NSW.

Bunda, T. (2014). *The relationship between Indigenous peoples and the university: Solid or what!* (Doctoral thesis). University of South Australia, Australia.

Gilbey, K. (2014). *Privileging First Nations knowledge: Looking back to move forward* (Doctoral thesis). Batchelor Institute of Indigenous Tertiary Education, Australia.

Harraway, D. (2016). *Staying with the trouble: Making kin in the Chthulucene*. Durham & London: Duke Press.

Heckenberg, R. (Creative Director). (2016). *Yindyamurra sculpture walk*. Murray River, NSW.

Kwaymullina, A. (2014). *Walking many worlds storytelling and writing for the Young*. Retrieved from www.wheelercentre.com/notes/ee221876968a8/

Kwaymullina, A. (2015). *Let the stories in: On power, privilege and being an Indigenous writer*. Retrieved from www.wheelercentre.com/notes/let-the-stories-in-on-power-privilege-and-being-an-indigenous-writer

Moreton, R. (2006). *The right to dream* (Doctoral thesis). University of Western Sydney, Australia.

Mountz, A., Bonds, A., Mansfield, B., Lloyd, J., Hyndman, J., Walton-Roberts, M., . . . Curran, W. (2015). For slow scholarship: A feminist politics of resistance through collective action in the neoliberal university. *ACME: An International Journal for Critical Geographies, 14*(4), 1235–1259.

Okri, B. (1997). *A way of being free*. London: Phoenix.

Ration Shed Museum Initiative. (n.d.). *The Cherbourg Memory*. Retrieved from http://cherbourgmemory.org

Riddle, S., Harmes, M., & Danaher, P. A. (Eds.). (2017). *Producing pleasure within the contemporary university*. Rotterdam: Sense Publishing.

The Women Who Write. (n.d.). *We are 'the women who write'*. Retrieved from www.thewomenwhowrite.com/about.html

Worby, G., Tur, S. U., & Rosas Blanch, F. (2014). Writing forward, writing back, writing black – Working process and work-in-progress. *Journal of the Association for the Study of Australian Literature, 14*(3), 1–14.

# Index

Page numbers in italic indicate a figure on the corresponding page.

Printed in the United States
by Baker & Taylor Publisher Services